PEYTON

*The World's Greatest
Yachting Cartoonist*

Kath Peyton

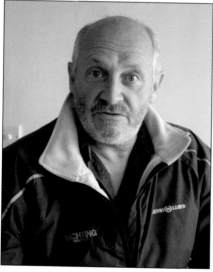

Dick Durham

Mike Peyton

PEYTON

The World's Greatest Yachting Cartoonist

Dick Durham

ADLARD COLES NAUTICAL
LONDON

For Katie

Published by Adlard Coles Nautical
an imprint of A & C Black Publishers Ltd
36 Soho Square, London W1D 3QY
www.adlardcoles.com

ISBN 978-1-4081-2440-6

A CIP catalogue record for this book is available from the
British Library.

This book is produced using paper that is made from wood grown in
managed, sustainable forests. It is natural, renewable and recyclable.
The logging and manufacturing processes conform to the environmental
regulations of the country of origin.

Designed by Susan McIntyre
Typeset in 10pt on 12pt Celeste

Printed and bound in China by C&C Offset Printing Co

• Contents •

• *Acknowledgements* •

I would like to thank Kath Peyton who made available to me her unpublished contemporary notes and diaries about the early years she spent with Mike, both when they met at art school and the sailing they went on to do together. All the other sailors, friends and relatives who have helped with Mike's story are mentioned as the yarn unfolds: my thanks to you all.

• *Photography credits* •

Danny Bray: p. 130i
Chris Doyle: p. 108
Dick Durham: pp. 1, 5, 13i, 47, 50, 63, 72, 97, 112, 113,
    129, 130ii, 131, 149, 150, 154, 155, 159, 160, 161, 162,
    163, 164, 165
Peter Firmin: pp. 35, 36
Paul Gelder: p. 80
Ian Griffiths: pp. 115, 117, 122, 123
Eric Hiscock: p. 68
Carlo Metzler: p. 151
Nick Newman: p. viii
Mike Peyton: pp. 8, 9, 13ii, 17, 18, 19, 31, 40, 41, 42, 44,
    45, 55, 56, 65, 69, 84, 89, 114, 132, 137, 139, 146, 155,
    156
Graham Snook: pp. 142, 143
Paul Tobias: pp. 73, 110

• *Foreword* •

Nick Newman is one of Britain's leading cartoonists who works for the *Sunday Times*, *Private Eye* magazine, *The Spectator* and *Yachting Monthly* among other titles. He was inspired to get involved in the inky trade by poring over Mike Peyton's cartoons as a youngster.

The first (and only) time I met Mike Peyton was at a *Yachting Monthly* Christmas party. For 30 years I had been in awe of him – he could draw the sea like nobody else, he was annoyingly funny, and my dad thought he was the best. When I was introduced to him as a fellow scribbler, he tried to kick my shins. I knew instantly that he was everything I aspired to be.

I've admired his work for as long as I can remember. My father had bought a labour-intensive yacht (a SCOD – South Coast One Design) and most school holidays seemed to involve scraping down green gloop, sandpapering until knuckles bled, and varnishing hopelessly. The only light relief at the end of the day was thumbing through the collections of Peyton cartoon books that my brother and I had bought for my dad every Christmas since time immemorial. But come Boxing Day, they would only remind my father that there was a keel to de-barnacle. Thanks, Mike.

The trouble with Peyton cartoons was that they weren't just funny – they were TRUE – which is the essence of great comedy. Not only were they beautifully drawn, they reflected the angst of sailing in all its depressing and liberating glory. Unlike those of us who haven't stepped on a yacht since 1974, Mike Peyton knows boats. The rigging, the mast-y business, the jib'n'spinnaker stuff that I could never understand, and the way that sailors invariably shout a lot and fall in the water at some stage or other. If it's happened to you, Mike Peyton has been there too. Maybe he even invented it.

Of course, sailing was not enough, and he had to extend his talents to *The New Scientist*. My fellow office cartoonist, David Austin, was a colleague of Mike's, and recounted stories of sailing trips – and also Mike's wartime reminiscences – which left the rest of us slack-jawed. This biography tells the tale.

As a cartoonist, I can say unequivocally that I hate Mike Peyton (and not just because of my bruised shins). He's better at observational comedy than most practitioners of the art, and has an eye for nautical detail that J M W Turner would admire.

Peyton also inspired one fledgling cartoonist to pick up a pen, and draw – and for that, thanks.

And ouch!

Nick Newman

• Books by Mike Peyton •

Early paperbacks
Ever Wonder Why We Do It?
Come Sailing with Peyton
Come Sailing Again
Best of Peyton

Later paperbacks
Quality Time, 2005
Floating Assets, 2008, (Adlard Coles
  Nautical)
Ever Wonder Why We Do It?, 2008,
  (Adlard Coles Nautical)
Out of Our Depth, 2009 (Adlard
  Coles Nautical)

Hardbacks
Finish With Engines, 1970
Come Sailing, 1975
Come Sailing Again, 1976
Hurricane Zoe and Other Sailing, 1977
They Call It Sailing, 1981
The Pick of Peyton, 1983
Out of Our Depth, 1985
Imminent in All Areas, 1987
Home and Dry, 1989

Non sailing
To Horse, 1980
Ski with Peyton, 1985
*An Average War, from Eighth Army
  to Red Army*, 2006

• Also by Dick Durham •

The Last Sailorman, Terence Dalton, 1989
On & Offshore: Cruising the Thames and the East Coast,
  Ashford Press Publishing, 1989
Where the River Meets the Sea, St Edmundsbury Press, 1991
The Magician of the Swatchways, Yachting Monthly, IPC Magazines, 1994

• *Preface* •

As features editor of *Yachting Monthly* magazine I'd gone along to interview the world's most famous marine cartoonist, and the tide was out. The River Blackwater had abandoned Maldon, Essex, leaving the salt-encrusted town stranded at the top of a glistening, muddy ditch. An ancient hill supporting the white clapboard tower of St Mary's Church overlooked Downs Road Boatyard, which appeared to double as a builder's yard. The tarpaulin-covered wooden boats with bared ribs, held precariously upright with props, shared the yard with piles of sand, torn down brick walls covered in tiles and an assortment of china WCs. Unshipped masts were stacked on racks which also held steel girders.

Then, between the boat carcasses under canvas shrouds awaiting buyers with enough faith to believe they could be resurrected, I spotted a figure. A white-haired man dressed in a navy blue fleece and jeans and carrying what appeared to be an old brown shopping bag walked down the hill towards me. Suddenly he stopped, bent over, and plucked a length of muddy rope from a frosty puddle. Oblivious to the February morning he shook the rope free of dirt, coiled it neatly and, carrying the rope in one hand and the bag in the other, continued down the hill and into the boatyard. He disappeared momentarily, behind a chocked up yacht, then re-appeared weaving between oil drums, holding rain water at waist height, rusting engine blocks, and an abandoned fridge, and started down the matchstick jetty alongside which lay the grey, 38 ft concrete hull of *Touchstone* on the deck of which I was waiting.

Touchstone at Downs Road Boatyard, Maldon, Essex

My first sight of Mike Peyton was reassuring. There was something deliberate, yet thoughtful about his approach. He was nothing like the thousands of fallible characters in woolly hats he'd created in over 60 years of drawing.

He hurled the muddy coil of rope onto *Touchstone*'s deck with a thud and then nimbly grabbed the port rigging and stepped onto the top of a giant dagger keel which was hauled up above the deck, and, using it as a gangway, swung himself aboard.

'Morning. You must be Mike?' I said with a friendly grin.

A baleful-looking face with large, bright blue eyes focused behind spectacles turned to mine. 'I'll get a fire goin,' he said with a heavy northern accent and disappeared below into an unlocked cabin.

There was no suggestion the sea was ever going to come back. Ricketty jetties pushed out into glutinous mud. All boats sat upright, stiff and still, deserted by the element their creators had designed them for. A wandering finger of tide was being pushed weakly back in by a North Sea neutered by neaps. There was plenty of time to light the coal stove, which had a crooked chimney, and to make bacon and eggs, Mike said.

Down below, *Touchstone* was a gloomy sarcophagus. In the chilly, damp air I half expected to find a mummified old salt from yesteryear lying in the coffin-like berths. The lack of light wasn't helped by a plywood, upside-down dinghy which covered the sky-light.

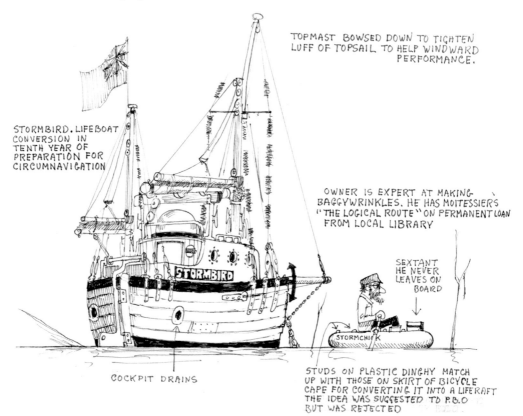

TOPMAST BOWSED DOWN TO TIGHTEN LUFF OF TOPSAIL TO HELP WINDWARD PERFORMANCE.

STORMBIRD. LIFEBOAT CONVERSION IN TENTH YEAR OF PREPARATION FOR CIRCUMNAVIGATION

OWNER IS EXPERT AT MAKING BAGGYWRINKLES. HE HAS MOITESSIER'S "THE LOGICAL ROUTE" ON PERMANENT LOAN FROM LOCAL LIBRARY

SEXTANT HE NEVER LEAVES ON BOARD

STORMBIRD

STORMCHICK

COCKPIT DRAINS

STUDS ON PLASTIC DINGHY MATCH UP WITH THOSE ON SKIRT OF BICYCLE CAPE FOR CONVERTING IT INTO A LIFERAFT THE IDEA WAS SUGGESTED TO P.B.O BUT WAS REJECTED

As a material for the construction of boats, ferro-cement is an obfuscation. For it is only ferro-cement while it's still in the sack. Once it's mixed with water, and aggregate, a necessary process to make an object, there's no getting away from it, it's concrete.

Mike and I remained standing in *Touchstone*'s saloon – it was too cold to sit down – with our coats zipped up to the neck, and hovered round the blackened stove waiting for the flickering flames to take hold of the coal and give off some heat.

'Concrete was the only material cheap enough to give me a boat of this length,' said Mike, 'she's got eight berths,' he added in his peculiarly high-pitched northern accent. I noticed he was quite happy to refer to his yacht as being concrete and not ferro-cement. Not a man given to euphemism, I thought, although I later discovered he understood it well enough. It was a linguistic camouflage for hiding essential truths which is what so many of his hapless characters have done over many decades whether they be on yachts, skis or horses. Whether dressed in Army fatigues, Scout uniforms, or clergyman's robes. Whether fiddling with caravans, bicycles or lorries, his luckless figures have appeared in more than 30 journals from *Tatler* to *Modern Caravan*, *Commercial Motor* to the *Church of England Times*, *Swift* comic to the *New Scientist*.

As a sluggish brown slurry crawled towards *Touchstone*'s mud-spattered hull we were joined by Paul Gelder, editor of *Yachting Monthly*. He had driven 200 miles from his home in Emsworth, Hampshire. He had sailed with Mike before and like so many of Mike's charterers – the business he had run alongside his cartooning and which had supplied so much of his material – wanted to do so again in spite of being buried alive in *Touchstone*.

We tucked into welcome plates of eggs and bacon, Mike smacking his lips like a hungry schoolboy. If you'd put a cap on his tousled head, and slung a torn blazer over his youthful physique, this man in his mid-80s could have passed for Richmal Crompton's 'William'.

After breakfast Mike looked at the slow tide. It was nigh on High Water. 'I don't think it's going to make much more. This breeze is holding it up,' he said. Certainly the limp tide could not be assisted in its approach by the near gale force south-westerly wind upon which herring gulls surfed across the big sky without flapping.

The tide, if that's what it really was, stopped: a sheet of mud-speckled froth which we knew would hover for 20 minutes before retreating once more, dragged back to sea by a moon fearful some of its off-white horses might be interred permanently in the ooze.

Touchstone's 8 ton hull did not budge an inch from the suck of the sticky river bed.

It looked as though I would have to do the interview in the Queen's Head on Hythe Quay under the shadow of the half dozen Thames spritsail barges that were moored there. Salvation arrived in the form of a white bearded man incongruously dressed in a royal blue boiler suit underneath a green Barbour jacket. At first glance I assumed he had arrived at Downs to attend to the sand, RSJs, or the demolished wall. But a Breton fisherman's cap caught my eye as Mike said: 'Hullo, Arthur, can we use your boat?'

Arthur Keeble, 73, did not answer which was clearly some sort of code for 'Yes' as Mike gestured to Paul and I to follow him down river to another precarious jetty alongside which was a smart-looking, long and narrow, pale blue 46 ft ketch called *Gem*. She, too, was concrete, but this one was afloat. Just.

'It's like Stonehenge round here,' said a woman, who I later learned was Mary, Arthur's wife. She remained on the jetty while the three of us joined Arthur aboard *Gem*. 'All these stone boats,' she added. I thought it was funny, but clearly the two concrete boat owners had heard the joke before as they did not laugh.

Soon we were underway at last, the strong wind and first of the ebb rushing *Gem* along at a healthy rate of knots past the barges, round Herring Point and into Colliers Reach. Paul and I wrestled with the tiller as the long boat skated this way and that on her way down to Osea Island while Arthur and Mike stood up on deck pulling down several reefs in the billowing tan mainsail. The pair of them stood to windward of the long boom as casually as though at a bus stop, and I feared the speeding boat – which I found difficult to keep straight – would gybe at any minute and throw my subject and his pal overboard.

That we were now on someone else's boat seemed random to Paul and I but I was to learn later on that Mike and his fellow sailors all operated like this. They referred to themselves, jokily, as the Flexible Yacht Club, for what was important was going sailing. It did not matter to where, with whom or in what.

Mike aboard *Gem*, another 'Stonehenge' boat   Arthur Keeble, '30 dossers' helped build his boat

'We'll take her over the land,' said Arthur mysteriously as we passed a pole sticking up out of the sea. It marked a wreck, appropriately enough a concrete wreck, the *Molliette*, a three-masted schooner built before World War 1. She had not been a success and now sat on a part of the sea bed ominously called the Cocum Hills.

It was so shallow that even when the dun-coloured waves broke, their crests were still beige. But soon we crossed into the deeper water of the River Colne and skimmed over the weak ebb tide, into Pyefleet Creek behind Mersea Island where we dropped anchor. This is Mike's favourite anchorage anywhere between the Baltic and the Mediterranean, I was to learn.

Gem in Pyefleet Creek, Mike's favourite anchorage

In *Gem*'s cabin I felt less like being entombed than I had aboard *Touchstone*. She was comfortable, clean and daylight had not been discouraged to enter.

Mike decided it was time for some more bacon and eggs. As he fried I asked Arthur how he started sailing. He was just a toddler when – complaining to his father that he would rather go paddling than be stuck on a 16 ft dayboat – his dad picked him up and dunked him over the side at Shore Ends on the River Crouch. '"Go paddling then," he said. My mother thought he was going to drown me.' Arthur went away to sea, gaining his master's ticket before becoming a skilled boat-builder, and a navigator on crack Fastnet race-boats: he taught navigation on the Hamble for many years and had been a yacht deliverer. If they were delivered by sea, Mike often crewed but if by land, then with the assistance of a home-made trailer built from two caravans. Arthur built *Gem* in the back garden of his home in Little Totham, Essex: 'I got 30 dossers to help me bucket in the cement,' he said. Arthur, I was to learn, was a typical Peyton shipmate: tough, silent and unorthodox. And, perhaps more importantly, good enough at sailing never to excite Mike's artistic antenna.

As he listened I noticed Mike had a curious habit of appearing to be – through a sudden rush of nostalgia – on the verge of an emotional outburst. His face was like the two masks of the theatre. I was not sure if he was going to laugh or cry and I willed him to do the former for decorum's sake.

As I got to know him – as I hope you will through the pages that follow – I think this peculiar demeanour when telling a funny, but poignant anecdote was, in the end, just an attempt to keep a lid on the sheer joy he felt looking back over his singular life.

He could hardly believe it himself.

Dick Durham

• 1 •

Benighted King Coal

Mike Peyton was born on 8th January 1921 in the shadow of the giant wheel which daily lowered cages carrying 1,705 miners, including Jeremiah, his father, into the bowels of County Durham, and his first memory is of disaster. In Houghton Colliery hewers, horse drivers, banksmen, putters, wastemen and timber erectors worked six days a week in poor light, 35°C heat and 90 per cent humidity, against coal seams as low as four feet in height.

Many years later, when swinging a lead line while plumbing modest depths to secure safe passage for his boat, Mike reflected on just how deep below ground his father had worked. The deepest pit was 780 feet deep, or 130 'fathoms' as his father used to say.

The colliery at Houghton-le-Spring, the ancient village five miles south of Sunderland, had claimed more than 140 lives by the time Mike was born. A further 16 would be killed before he started school. 'The pit had a 'hooter' which used blasts in a certain sequence to call all hands when there was an accident. When it hooted this special code all the adults left the room,' Mike said recalling this grim childhood memory, 'I began to realise the women went to the pit head to wring their hands and pray and the men went to see if they could help'.

The Sunderland Echo dutifully recorded the horrible deaths of its sons down in the stifling heat of the galleries. Flattened by falls of stone, blown apart from the ignition of coal dust from the ironically named safety lamps they carried, or crushed by de-railed coal tubs, their broken bodies were buried in the churchyard of St Michael and All Angels. The church also holds the tomb of Bernard Gilpin, the 16th century evangelising Archdeacon of Durham, who opened his doors to feed rich and poor alike. He was killed at the age of 66 after being knocked down by an oxen in the city's market. To this day oxen are roasted at the annual Houghton Feast in Sunderland. More than 525 years after Gilpin's death, Mike's eldest daughter, Hilary, runs a hog-roasting business in Essex. Too bad there was no Bernard Gilpin around to help the down-trodden miners of his home village three centuries later. For it was said the pit ponies were looked after better than the men at Houghton Colliery.

It might have been a dangerous and filthy job – Mike remembers his father washing off the coal dust in a galvanised bath each night as there were no pit head showers – but Jeremiah had lived in fear of the workhouse. Only a decade before Mike was born, 138 people lived in the Houghton-le-Spring Union Workhouse, some on 'lunatic wards' that included a padded room. The hard-drinking Jeremiah was determined Mike was not going to follow in his footsteps and when his son was a teenager he took him down the pit giving him a tour that he would never forget.

As he made his way to the pit each day, Jeremiah was spotted from his peculiar gait. He threw his right leg forward with each step before planting it on the cobbles,

We don't know where We're goin' But We're on our way.

Far right: Jeremiah Peyton, Mike's father, wounded three times in Flanders

as he still carried shrapnel in it from three separate wounds suffered while fighting with the Garrison Artillery in the trenches of Flanders during World War 1. Before the war he had been accepted as a police officer by the local constabulary: his escape from the cages of Houghton Colliery. After the war, with a leg too gammy for the police, he was glad the pit would take him back. The specialist Austrian doctor who tried to operate on his leg was based in Glasgow where Jeremiah met another casualty of the Great War. He was a professional singer who had been wounded in the throat. 'Dad said he was so scared he would not be able to sing any more that when he tried his voice out he talked the words: "Let the great big world keep turning" before trying to sing them,' said Mike.

Jeremiah thought nothing of his misfortune: after all his wife Emily had lost her first husband, John Kells – one of five brothers, all killed, three on the same day – in that war. Just how effective the Pals' Battalions had been as a recruitment device by getting men to join up with their mates was only fully realised after the war when men's names were erased from the electoral role and instead listed neatly in stone. When Mike returned wearing his own Army uniform to visit his grandma, 'she was always dressed in black', only later did he realise the feelings of doom she must have harboured seeing him about to go off to another war.

Emily had given birth to a son from her first marriage: Tom, who was born three years before Mike. As well as Mike, Emily and Jeremiah had a daughter, Mary, born five years after Mike.

In 1925 Lambton, Hetton and Joicey Collieries, owners of Houghton pit, decided along with Britain's other mine-owners to reduce the comparatively well-paid miners' wages and increase their working day to improve production and cut costs. The Government set up a Royal Commission to look into the problems of the mining industry. It, too, recommended the miners' pay be cut. By the following year the mine-owners announced a wage cut of between 10 and 25 per cent. If the miners did not accept their new terms of employment, then from 1 May, they would be locked out of the pits.

On the 3rd of May, the General Strike was called by the Trades Union Council for other industries to support the miners. Nearly five million men came out in the biggest strike in Britain's history to date. Although the strike only lasted nine days, the coal mine stoppage continued until November.

If times had always been tough for the Peyton family they now got a whole lot tougher. With three children to feed 'food was always short' anyway. Now they were close to starving.

Tom and Mike would push Mary in a pram around the district. The pram had a well beneath the bed board and, lifting Mary out, the boys would fill this cavity with swedes 'gleaned' from local fields.

Such continual hunger and privation would never be forgotten by Mike who cannot leave a scrap of food uneaten on his plate to this day.

The Peyton family decided enough was enough and before the end of 1926 moved down to Emily's mother's home in Radcliffe, just north of Manchester, where they hoped Jeremiah could find work.

They packed their belongings and said goodbye to Houghton-le-Spring, its cemeteries full of dead miners, its war memorial, and crossed the Pennines into Lancashire and life.

Mike Peyton (left) and Tom Peyton pushed their sister Mary around town in a pram

Left behind in the backyard of their old home, across the fields from the colliery, was a faint line scratched in the dirt. It was a shallow trench Mike had dug for his lead toy soldiers. He lined them up along the edge facing the lifting gear of Houghton Colliery and left them out in all weathers. As the rain fell his mother told him the paint would wash off. 'That's what happens to real soldiers,' said five-year-old Mike, perhaps making his earliest reference to an interest in roughing it.

It was certainly his first experience of manipulating small figures.

• 2 •

The North

Hurtling round the M25 in my battered people carrier, large, blue motorway signs flashed past announcing the approach of the M1. My passenger, Mike Peyton, read the last one before we peeled off: 'The North,' he said, 'it's such an evocative phrase'. Though he had headed south more than 50 years before, the town of his youth was still deeply embedded in his soul.

We left the M1, with its dusty fox corpses littered along the hard shoulder, at the Sheffield turning and started climbing up over the southern tail of the Pennines, stopping for a lunch of giant beef sandwiches at the Ladybower pub in the desolate peaks. The car park was packed and the bar full of hearty hikers, male and female, all shod in serious-looking footwear. 'They drive out to these places and take off into the hills,' Mike explained. After lunch we drove down through Snake Pass and into Glossop where, as we shuffled through the traffic, Mike noticed the passing garish shopfront signs for pizzas, deep-fried chicken and burgers. 'Years ago the only sign you saw round here was UCP...United Cow Products,' Mike recalled. Tripe, lights, and sweetbread: the fast food of a lost world.

The back of Mike's sister's two-bedroom, semi-detached home in Radcliffe looks east towards the alluring Derbyshire Peaks which were to draw Mike away as a teenager on his first adventures.

Mary, a friendly, intelligent woman, is sharp-witted and funny: virtues honed by the banter of the street markets she worked in all her life. Our hastily arranged visit had coincided with the arrival of her daughter Bernadette, a special needs teacher from Hertford, but neither Mary nor her husband Bill, a retired plumber, were put out. Bernadette was simply given a neighbour's room for the night. In time-honoured northern fashion, neighbours kept 'open house' for neighbours.

With a gate-legged table extended to make room for three extra settings, Mary produced a delicious stew and I produced a bottle of red wine from the Asda store, a mile away, which has replaced the local shops which once stood in Mary's street, and sat back to hear about Mike's early life. Both Mary and her daughter declined a drink, leaving the wine for their menfolk: a system of patriarchy still more marked north of Watford than south of it.

The family were brought up as Roman Catholics, although, after his experiences in the trenches, Jeremiah's faith was never as strong as his wife's. His stepson, Tom, was a willing altar boy, but Mike's and Mary's intellect was drawn more towards science than sacrament.

'It does come in handy, though, being Roman Catholic, especially when the Jehovah's Witnesses come to the door,' said Mary. As children they were expected by their mother to attend church and when the local priest said he wanted all children to make their confessions in the morning, Mary answered: 'I didn't commit any sins until this afternoon.'

Before the family arrived in Radcliffe in 1926, all talk concerning Lancashire had been about the mills and the work they would supply, so when Mike first saw the grimy, brick chimneys which dominated the skyline, he was disappointed: he had expected windmills.

Mike can still hear the noise from the steel-soled clogs of the mill-working girls as they walked the cobbled streets of Radcliffe on their way to work in the morning, kicking up sparks before dawn as they set off to manufacture the world's textiles.

When the hard-working citizens of Radcliffe gave up the ghost they were laid out in their coffins and put on display in the parlours of the terraced houses. Anyone could come and pay their last respects. Children, of course, were naturally fascinated to see their neighbours dead. 'I remember old Ruby,' said Mary, 'she died and we knocked on the door and said: "can we come in and see her?".' Her daughter told us: "If you see her you've got to pray."'

At the local funeral directors, Mike and Mary liked to ask: 'Got any empty boxes?' for a laugh. But as soon as he was old enough Mike took on various Saturday jobs, one of which was delivering wreaths for the undertaker he had mocked. He also started carrying a notepad and a Black Prince pencil with him at all times. 'You used to sit at night after school and ask me to draw a line or a circle and you would draw me something,' said Mary. I handed her my notebook and Mary drew the letter 'Z' on an angle, then turned it into a dog's face. 'Like that, he would. I'd have given anything to draw like you,' she said. Mike then took my notebook and turned two letter Cs – one inverted – into a robin.

Mike was given a straight edge – from the funeral director he worked for – to help with his drawings. He still has it.

At the local Catholic school, St Mary's, Mike's teacher asked the class to draw the owl and the pussycat, Mary recalled. 'You drew a picture and she said you'd traced it. She kept you in to draw it again.'

Such punishment had their mother Emily up at the school: 'If you want him to draw it again, he can do it at home, not at school. He doesn't tell lies,' she said, although she admonished her son when he started running away from the injustice of the classroom. Mike found solace in the escapism provided by *Rover*, *Adventure* and *Wizard* comics. He loved the figures hanging for dear life on the backs of speeding cars, climbing along the roofs of thundering trains, or wing-walking on swooping bi-planes. He followed the characters from box to box as they fought with grizzly bears, climbed treacherous mountains, or battled stormy seas. It seemed to him that man was an accident waiting to happen in a world of adventure readily available in the great outdoors, or at the mercy of thrills produced by the technology of transport. It was a world where the Mounties always got their man, robots had human characteristics, and David of the local football club beat Goliath of the First Division.

Mike and Mary once went to see the *Bride of Frankenstein* at the local cinema. 'During the interval I could see you drawing,' said Mary, 'and I'd been sitting there scared out me wits'. Mike was starting to draw his own adventure characters. He also loved reading Zane Grey's violent western adventure stories such as *The Lone*

Star Ranger, and *Riders of the Purple Sage*. And his first sketches were of cowboys and horses.

His early passion for books was little to do with the school: 'You got me onto the William books,' he told Mary, 'so I blame you for my crime reading'. Mike and another lad were top of the class at their Catholic school but they were not altar boys and once it was clear they weren't bound for the priesthood, lesser pupils got scholarships to go to the Catholic grammar school over their heads. It was something that Mike always resented and it put him off religion for life.

His schooling finished when he was 13, and as his mother put it succinctly: 'He left school before he knew what he was capable of'.

He was interviewed for a job at the local brewery where, upon hearing his name, his potential employer asked: 'Are you Irish?'

'No, but me dad is,' came Mike's artless reply.

Jeremiah, known as 'Derby' by his wife who found his real name a mouthful, had secured employment as a labourer in a coconut matting factory. His job was to roll the huge bales of matting from the production line to waiting lorries. 'His hands blew up like puddings,' Mike said, but he'd earned enough to help Mike buy his first pushbike.

'Cycling was what we all did. There were at least five cycling clubs in Radcliffe. We would set off at the weekends and cycle anywhere within 50 miles.'

Tea shops sprang up to cater for the new craze and triangular race courses of up to 100 miles were set up and watched by those cyclists who were less competitive. But as races were not allowed on the public highway, the contestants would set off at two minute intervals, the elapsed times to be worked out later. When the Youth Hostels started, the cyclists could stay overnight at weekends at fourpence a time. His bicycle got long and hard use and at one time the front forks sheared off and Mike went down on his face, fracturing his skull. At Preston Infirmary he was wheeled on a trolley down a corridor passing his parents who walked straight past, not recognising their son as he was bandaged up 'like a mummy'.

For his holidays Mike cycled back to Houghton-le-Spring to visit his uncle John who was a soldier in the Northumberland Fusiliers and who had been a personal bodyguard to the Prince of Wales. As such he'd spent much time in London and fired his teenage nephew's imagination about the capital.

The roads took Mike over the moors, and he began to feel drawn to the wilderness passing him by on each side. All the mill towns were in valleys, where the water was harnessed for power, so to explore the moors meant walking out of town and up into the hills which supported the moors on their summits. He bought a stiff pair of boots and started 'bog-trotting' as hill walking was called, getting the bus back at the end of a day's hike. Rambling far and wide over the peat and rock of the Pennines was a lot more pioneering than sticking to the straight and narrow metalled road hoping that, mile after mile, round the next bend would be an adventure he could be an accident in.

But Mike also wanted to see the fabled London his uncle had mentioned. So he sold his pushbike and hitchhiked to the capital arriving in Hammersmith where he was arrested. 'If you were called Mick or Paddy, then, you were Irish and possibly IRA Irish,' Mary said. Mike managed to convince the London's guardians that the toothbrush in his pocket was for nothing more sinister than oral hygiene, and was released.

Mike, his sister Mary and her husband Bill

Emily, Mike's mother and his half brother Tom

By now Mike had a dead-end job working in a rubber factory. Each day he walked along a road of terraced houses at the end of which was a long, high, brick wall. The routine was monotonous and he counted the bricks along the wall and one day gave himself a deadline. 'I said to myself when I reach the last brick in the wall, my life's going to change and I'm going to change it.' At the end of the wall he turned a corner and spotted a chain-driven lorry about to leave the rubber works: 'Tell my mother I won't be home for lunch,' he said to a workmate and approached the lorry driver. Minutes later he was on his way to Wales where he spent several days walking in the hills, sleeping at night in barns or haystacks.

He was moving from box to box in his own, real-life adventure.

The family put his wanderlust down to his father's elder brother, Michael, after whom he was named. He had disappeared and nobody knew where he was until one day a postcard arrived from Japan. Later, at the outbreak of World War 1, Michael had made his way to Halifax, Nova Scotia, where he joined the Royal Engineers as a Pioneer. He died on 26th March 1918 and is buried in the town's Mount Olivet Cemetery, a victim of disease or killed in a training exercise, the family are not sure which.

It was conflict which brought the chance of serious adventure in the great outdoors for Mike, when on 3rd September 1939 Britain declared war on Hitler's Germany. He was turned down by the Royal Navy because his eyesight wasn't good enough, he did not even try the RAF because he felt his lack of education would hold him back, so instead he went round Army recruitment offices. Mike, then 18, discovered he would have to wait until he was 20 to be allowed overseas to fight. One of Radcliffe's cotton mills had been converted into an office for administering the affairs of the Army Pay Corps, 'but I wanted the red flash of the infantry on my uniform,' said Mike. As towns turned all lights off after dark so as not to assist the Luftwaffe, Saturday nights out in Manchester at the skating rink or the Palais dance hall, where couples swirled to singer Ivor Novello or the all-girl dance band of Ivy Benson, were 'a pleasurable contrast especially if you had a female companion'.

Mike became fascinated by the cartoon run in one newspaper titled, *Heard in the Blackout*: it was simply a black square carrying the quotes of the myopic victim beneath. By now he was attending evening classes in drawing two nights a week. Influences that would help him create his own cartoon characters would soon come to fruition.

He would often take Mary into Manchester and once, at the Ritz, told her to sit back and watch him dance. Mike had been encouraged by his father to learn ballroom dancing. Jeremiah had been denied the pleasure after suffering his war wounds, but he would sit and watch the dancers enjoying themselves. Mary recalls overhearing some girls in the ladies' loo, when Mike took her to one ballroom. 'They were saying "He int' half a case he int" and "he's a right fool he is" and I knew they were talking about you,' she said.

At the recruiting office in Manchester's Albert Square, Mike told the clerk he wanted to join the Northumberland Fusiliers as at least one member of his family had long been in that regiment. 'A good mob. They relieved us at Loos,' the clerk said recalling his own fighting during World War 1. Mike received his call up papers on 16th October 1940. He was 19.

A chilly, damp morning greeted Mike and I as we prepared to leave Radcliffe. Mary said she didn't think she'd make it down to Mike's Essex home any more as Bill's stroke had affected his motor abilities, though clearly not his mind.

'We're all fraying round the edges, Mary,' Mike said, and suggested he and I had a look at the old family home in Radcliffe before heading south.

'They've knocked it down, they're knocking down the church too,' said Mary, 'and the school's been turned into an old folks' home, so there's no blue plaque for Mike Peyton anywhere.'

Mike paused then said: 'You're the only bit of Radcliffe left, Mary...I just got out in time'. We headed back to the motorway.

• 3 •

The Mickey Mouse Club

The Northumberland Fusiliers depot was in Newcastle: almost childhood territory for the rookie soldier. On his old home ground there were still family and many friends for Mike to call upon. He spent seven months in Fenham Barracks learning how to dismantle and re-assemble a Vickers machine-gun. Though he never used one in anger, to this day his training has stayed with him. 'Even now if I have to judge weight I start with 40 pounds – the weight of a Vickers machine-gun tripod – and go up or down from that.' Though the repetitive and finely detailed training with the gun was never required to face the enemy, such rigour and attention to detail saved the lives of Mike and some of his unit one night when a drunken fusilier woke up and went berserk. He fixed a bayonet to his loaded rifle and charged his mates, screaming 'I'll get one of you fuckers,' but tripped over a block of wood screwed to the barracks floor to stop the Vickers tripod moving about during training. He was disarmed by Mike and the others and taken back to his bunk. This time he slept as they had beaten him unconscious. Such early army life inspired the first of Mike's cartoons.

The class system, so entrenched in English society in the 1940s, was magnified in such a necessarily hierarchical organisation as the army. 'Accent was all, and the right one signified education. Even the NCOs who instructed us, showed deference to those they knew would get commissions.'

Mike and his flat northern accent, which even today his pals attempt to mimic, was drafted to join the Fourth Battalion of the Northumberland Fusiliers, a territorial unit who had a nickname: The Abington Mashers, named after the location of their annual camp where drink was taken. They had a theme tune, too.

This is how it went:

> *We are the Abington Mashers*
> *We go every night on the mash*
> *And when we can't get any beer*
> *It's all for the want of some cash.*
> *We can dance we can sing,*
> *We're all right, all right*
> *When we're tight, tight, tight,*
> *We don't give a damn for tomorrow*
> *What we ain't got we can borrow*
> *All that we require is beer, baccy and c****

With the Abington Mashers, Mike was posted to Shepton Mallet in Somerset to join 12 Platoon, Z Company. The mashers had to get used to cider instead of beer. It was a lot cheaper so the effects of mashing were felt sooner in the evening than later.

Mike sailed to war aboard the *Arundel Castle* from Newport to Port Tewfik, at the southern end of the Suez Canal in Egypt. One of the dignitaries aboard ship was the exiled Emperor of Abyssinia, Haile Selassie, on his way back to his capital, Addis Ababa, regained by the Allies five years after the Italians had invaded it. Mike recalls him as being: 'a tiny, bearded man who always wore a black cloak and who walked round the upper decks for exercise'. The ship had been in an escorted convoy and gone the long way round – around the Cape of Good Hope – to avoid German U-Boats, but when other troops joined them at Freetown, Sierra Leone, they discovered one of the ships had been torpedoed.

All Mike's letters home during the war years were signed 'Mick'. It was only later in life he changed it to Mike, to avoid being associated with the Republican Irish, once the Troubles re-surfaced.

At Port Tewfik hundreds of cawing jackdaws descended on the upperworks of the *Arundel Castle* to herald dusk. As the searing sun went down, a British destroyer slid into dock with torn and twisted hull plating, guns knocked askew and with ragged holes in her superstructure. 'She had been in the wars...we had arrived,' said Mike.

They disembarked at Port Tewfik and were shocked with their first experiences of the east: squatter latrines, markets full of butchered animals: their heads – still with glazed eyes wide open – laid out neatly in bloody rows, and the eerie wail of the muzzein.

Fears that Hitler would move on Cyprus following his success taking Crete in May 1941 saw Mike and his unit embarked for a sea passage to Limassol. During the voyage Mike turned in on deck beneath a lifeboat. Rough weather shifted some army vehicles in the hold and the ship took on a list. When Mike awoke he discovered it was only four inches of toe rail that had prevented him becoming lost overboard.

Sleeping off duty was one thing, but while on guard duty it was punishable by court martial and – during his father's war – sometimes death. So one moonlit night while Mike was on guard he was grateful of the company of a hedgehog to help him from nodding off. 'He came snuffling along on his nocturnal travels and I touched him with my bayonet and immediately he curled up into a ball.' This was repeated for the next two hours as the creature danced with Mike's bayonet, and when it was over, Mike rolled the hedgehog back into the safety of the ditch from where he'd emerged.

In November 1941, Mike's phoney war ended when his unit left Cyprus aboard a mine-laying cruiser, HMS *Abdiel*, which landed them at Haifa, in British Mandated Palestine. From here they went overland into 'the Blue' as the soldiers called the Western Desert. Some officers of his battalion went on ahead to see what they could expect. One of those 'going point' was to the naïve young Mike's eyes the 'epitome of an officer': tall, dark, with the arrogant self-confidence acquired at a public school: the type of education denied of Mike. He had a thick, dark moustache to give a touch of maturity to his young face and an accent designed to 'rally the ranks when the Gatlin jammed'. But whatever it was he witnessed up in 'the Blue' had compromised such demeanour. The officer conveniently discovered he was shortsighted and was shipped back to Britain. 'We later heard he had become a desert expert, as one would expect of a man of his character.'

Mike's first brush with the enemy was when he himself was going into 'the Blue'

Mike, left, in Cyprus, 1941

while on a patrol. He was suddenly confronted by a truck with a mounted machine-gun packed with armed soldiers driving towards him at speed. They were Italians who had being lying in a wadi waiting for a surrender window. Mike seemed like a good bloke to surrender to and not a shot was fired. Mike's youngest daughter Veronica told me 68 years later that her father still despised Italians 'because they were such useless soldiers'.

As they rounded up their swarthy prisoners, the Abington Mashers found a box of medals that had been cast ready to distribute to victorious Italians once they'd taken Cairo. The mashers lined the Italians up for an awards ceremony and decorated them with the gongs before marching them back into the Allied lines. The mashers' next visitation from the Roman enemy was more sombre. Various platoons had been given time off to go for a swim in the Mediterranean. But all thoughts of taking a dip evaporated in the desert heat when they were confronted by scores of Italian corpses washing up on the beach from a sunken troopship. 'Lining the shore were bloated bodies straining at their lifejackets with more arriving every minute.' The swimming party became a burial detail spawning a typical masher response: 'Fall in 12 Platoon for a bathing parade – bring your shovels'.

In January 1942 the battalion were driven in cattle trucks to Syria, and Mike's aesthetic eye fell upon the astonishing sight of cavalry: 'All the horses were being ridden bareback and the sunburnt riders hadn't a shirt between them. Both horses and riders merged in shades of brown so that they seemed almost as one...it was a kaleidoscope of rearing, wheeling, kicking life and movement'. It was like a scene from a Zane Grey novel and one of several that Mike illustrated his prolific letters home with.

Before his family saw them, Mike's sketches were enjoyed by the censor who alerted an intelligence officer on the lookout for someone with an aptitude for

Mike, right, Egypt, 1941

drawing to work on the situation map. Mike got the job. 'I am probably still alive through it,' he said, 'friend and foe would be crayoned in, the opposition in black and ourselves in red. The names of the opposition soon became familiar to me, the 21st Panzer, the 90th Light, the Ariete, the Trento, the Littorio. I became a man with information.'

It was at this time that the role of the battalion was changed, too. It became part of the Support Group of the 22nd Armoured Division: a kind of mobile fort used to harbour tanks, artillery and Bren gun carriers. As part of this re-organisation, Mike went off to Brigade HQ to work in Intelligence.

The mobile fort: armoured vehicles and fighting units on the outside, moved in a box shape, protecting the soft vehicles – lorries, ambulances, mobile workshops – within it. It took more than 1,000 vehicles to move a brigade and in the desert compass bearings were the 'roads' along which it travelled.

'Travelling across the desert was like travelling at sea. It was flat and pretty near featureless and it could be tricky, but if you had a landmark or two – a knocked out tank, a crashed plane or a grave – the job would be easy. It paid to notice at what angle you passed these landmarks for the return trip,' said Mike. He excelled in his new job and tried to join the Long Range Desert Group, the 'taxi service' of the SAS, because of their specialised operations in desert navigation, and intelligence gathering far behind enemy lines. However he was told he could not leave the Support Group as he was 'essential to the well being of the Battalion'.

The first casualties sustained by the newly formed battalion happened after an attack by Kittihawk planes flown by South African forces who later sent a letter of apology. It was such friendly fire incidents that had the 8th Army dubbed the 'Mickey Mouse Club' by its fighters and not the 'Desert Rats', which was used by the press.

The first time Mike came under shellfire he remained upright and carried on walking as a group of Indian troops dived under a lorry for cover. 'Common sense told me I should have hit the deck, too, but I had been brought up on the standards of boys' magazines and the books of Biggles and Bulldog Drummond where Britons were a superior race who set the standards over "lesser breeds". It was a habit I speedily got out of after I experienced the concentrated viciousness and murderous power when a shell landed in the vicinity. And after you had seen what a shell could do to a man it needed a conscious effort of will to keep control of one's self.' Shellfire was indiscriminate.

Working with Intelligence meant Mike saw many POWs brought in for interrogation and was surprised to find that Italian soldiers had among their belongings two separate collections of pictures: the first was of madonnas, crucifixions and a variety of saints, the second 'more dog-eared pack' was of soft-porn postcards. Before they were returned to their owners, Mike mixed the two packs up. A more chilling feature of POW 'property' was found among the German prisoners. They had photographs of each other standing triumphantly at various battlefields and in the background were trucks loaded with corpses. When a German quartermaster's store was overrun on one sortie, Mike found a box of Soligen shaving razors. He used one to sharpen his drawing pencils.

Leave from the blue was enjoyed in Cairo where Mike saw *Gone with the Wind* at the cinema and where he visited an art exhibition that was combined with a lecture from New Zealand's official war artist Peter McIntyre. 'He talked about the difficulties he faced from the hard, straight line of the desert horizon that divided all his compositions. I appreciated what he meant, but thought that there were a lot of people up the blue who would have willingly swapped their problems for his.'

Until now, Mike's cartoons had been sketches of various experiences but without the injection of irony or humour. This changed when he crafted a drawing straight from an incident he'd witnessed of a soldier pushing at a door marked PULL. On the shoulder strap of the soldier's jacket was printed the word INTELLIGENCE. After the war it was the first ever cartoon he sold. It was published by *Soldier* magazine.

A patina of desert dust covered all surfaces and all food cooked in the blue had sand in it. 'I've heard men say, just as they would of salt, "It needs more sand in it" and sprinkle a pinch in their bully stew,' said Mike.

One morning in the desert Mike was asked to assist with a casualty who was lying on his back smoking a cigarette. A blanket was laid beside the man and, with Mike at his ankles and another soldier supporting his shoulders, they lifted the man onto the blanket. As he left the ground both his legs bent upwards and came off in Mike's hands. 'It was the greatest shock I ever received in my life, I put the legs down and was sick.' The now legless man kept on smoking. A piece of fine shrapnel had caused the surreal surgery.

Another incident of desert life was to provide Mike with a cartoon for *Horse & Hound* many years later. He and another soldier had a narrow escape near dusk when they heard the 'familiar rattling squeak of tanks approaching', which they assumed to be German. They took cover in a slit trench but wondered if

Mike, Cairo, 1942

they had been spotted and speculated as to what fate lay for POWs taken by tanks. They reasoned they would be an unwanted nuisance at which point Mike's companion asked him: 'What comes after "Our Father who art in heaven?"...' Mike replied that if he did not know that by now he did not deserve salvation. However they had not been seen and 'we lived to pray another day'. The theological question asked of Mike was used verbatim as a cartoon caption during a hazardous moment in a foxhunt. But readers of *Horse & Hound* complained it was blasphemous.

The pious readers might have approved of the attack made by the Gloucestershire Hussars that Mike saw. One tank commander, probably a *Horse & Hound* reader himself, was blowing a hunting horn. 'Whenever I hear the sound of a hunting horn echoing over the winter fields at home today that action is brought vividly to mind.'

Mike's Intelligence officer Lieutenant John Barnett was run over in his sleeping bag by a friendly tank and had his ribs crushed. He was fighting for breath and had gone blind. Mike sat with him re-telling Daphne du Maurier's story *Frenchman's Creek* – which they had both read – until he was taken off to a field hospital. Mike wondered what happened to him, until he ran into him 55 years later during a canal barge trip in Worcester. His sight had returned in a POW camp where he had received medical attention. Sixty-eight years later his widow, Margaret Barnett told me: 'Mike held his hand while John begged him to keep on talking. He did so until the first aiders came and John was always grateful for his kindness.'

Although compassion and assistance was readily available for those still living, for those who were dead there was no sentimentality as this snapshot of dialogue recorded by Mike, demonstrates:

'Henderson has just got the knock'
'Which Henderson?'
'Henderson 72'
'I wonder who's got his Lilo?'

By June 1942 Mike's work in Intelligence was over: 'The situation map looked pretty depressing, the red bits shrinking and the black gradually surrounding them.' He put down his pencil and picked up his rifle to help with the Support Group's orders to stay and fight a rearguard action as the 22nd Armoured Brigade was ordered to retreat.

After six days they ran out of ammunition and were overrun by German tanks and left just to torch their own trucks and other vehicles, before they were taken prisoner.

On the 6th June 1942 the 4th Battalion Royal Northumberland Fusiliers (50th Reconnaissance Unit) ceased to exist as an effective part of the military machine. Of the original 800 men of all ranks, just four officers and 106 men were left. This remnant fought a series of rearguard actions in the retreat to Alamein by which time there were only 40 men left.

As Mike poignantly put it: 'The Abington Mashers would go on the mash no more'.

• 4 •

Man Eating Dog

In the desert, prison camps required no fences, guards or watchtowers. Water, or lack of it, formed an invisible perimeter beyond which lay death from dehydration for would-be escapees. The Germans who took Mike prisoner left him lying on the sand for his first night's 'captivity' where he and a sergeant, Alf Thomson, from the County of London Yeomanry used their greatcoats, buttoned together, to shelter a wounded man dressed only in shorts. The next morning a German truck took the casualty and other wounded soldiers away while Mike tried to escape by lying in a slit trench covered in sand. He was soon discovered and the Germans then checked all slit trenches. They were trucked away to a transit camp in Tripoli, capital of Italy's colony Libya, which it had forcibly taken from the decaying Ottoman Empire just before World War 1. As they headed off west, Mike and sergeant Thomson saw two of their comrades lying in dark-stained sand. They had attempted to escape in the night and had trodden on mines. They were still alive.

In the Tripoli camp the internees grew weak from lack of enough food. As Mike sat listlessly under the shade of a tree one day, a scrap of newspaper blew along the ground. He picked it up and was amazed to discover it was an English newspaper, three years old, covering a football match between his home side Bury against Aston Villa. The serendipity of the moment was even more marked because Mike and his father had attended the match. 'I rarely went to football matches, but dad had taken me along to this one because for Bury it was a big signing of a new player called Kilshaw.' The caption to the picture on the torn scrap of newsprint read: 'Kilshaw making his debut for Bury and Aston Villa'.

With the sand beneath the feet too hot to walk upon, a form of mental escapism, if not actual liberation, came in the form of a book about an expedition to climb Nanda Devi, a Himalayan peak. The prisoners took it in turns to soak up the descriptions of snowfields, icefalls and blizzards. It sparked off a hankering in Mike to go climbing mountains; an adventure he would later realise.

Mike left the Maghreb on an Italian ship, down in the hold packed in with other prisoners. This human cargo was allowed a patch of blue sky as Italian soldiers stood guard over an open hatchway until a klaxon warned of a submarine attack. The ship's hatches were then battened down and the captives sat in the darkness grimly awaiting an ironic fate worthy of membership of the Mickey Mouse Club.

Few north-bound ships were attacked, however, as the Royal Navy knew only too well what they contained.

The ship docked at Naples and the prisoners were taken to a tented camp at Capua, where after an administrational cock-up, uncharacteristic of a dictator who had got the trains to run on time, some of the men were inoculated twice, a precaution which killed 26 of them.

They were then moved on to another camp near Ancona and housed in sheds with three-tiered bunk beds. Two thousand men were held in the camp that was only 40m x 40m square.

Mike's hard youth in the mining town of Houghton-le-Spring now stood him in good stead for the starvation rations meted out. Breakfast was a cup of sugarless black coffee, which was thought to have been made from acorns. Later in the morning a 'fist-sized bread roll and a finger of cheese' was distributed to each man. Supper was a pint of thin soup. At the first funeral of a dead prisoner, the camp turned out to show its last respects. But soon ten prisoners were dying each week and the sergeant major in charge of obsequies was told masher-style: 'stick him in the soup' when the hungry men were called upon to mourn.

At such a rate of attrition it did not take a mathematician to work out on which date the camp would be empty.

Among the walking skeletons were those with pot bellies, not the result of any favouritism but because they were suffering from beriberi, as well as malnutrition.

The men responded in two ways: either to walk continuously around the camp, or to remain in their bunks getting up only for roll call and food. They were called 'horizontal champions'. Mike was of the former group, believing it better to keep moving. The only conversation was about food. The men fantasised about it.

'The greatest thing that life could have offered me at that time would have been a tin of condensed milk and a spoon,' said Mike. An ex-chef among the men, Nobby Clark, was called upon to talk them through the making of a six-course meal, starting with shopping at the market, preparing the ingredients and then cooking them. The men sat round drooling, but the cry of 'Give us a six-course meal, Nobby' never failed to gather a crowd.

Each man took it in turns to gather the day's bread ration in his blanket and after it had been distributed he had the bonus of combing the woollen sheet for crumbs. One prisoner searched the grass patch under the perimeter wire for snails. At one stage even the nutritious properties of the lice infesting the men's clothing was considered. But they were too small to be worth harvesting for the pot.

It came as something of a diversion, especially for Mike, when a former art teacher, Paul Bullard, started running life classes. Cigarettes had become camp currency and Mike used his to buy paper and pencils. Bullard used his to 'pay' for emaciated prisoners to act as models. 'You'll get as fine a knowledge here of bone construction as anywhere else in the world,' he said without irony. Mike recalls pointing out the beauty of the snow-covered peaks of the distant Apennines to Bullard. In reply this remarkable man discussed the translucent colours inside an empty salmon tin.

The supply of paper was also used by an ex-journalist to start a 'wall newspaper'. It had news snippets, profiles on internees and their civilian occupations, sketches from Bullard of Jacob wrestling with the angels, an obituary column, and cartoons from Mike.

When boxes of hoped-for food from the Vatican turned out to be full of accordions, the men were furious: they didn't have the strength to play them anyway! But, as ever, there were those who looked positively on hardship and it was suggested that a man playing an accordion would raise morale and that he could have an extra ration to do so. Competition for the job was fierce.

As Red Cross parcels arrived, albeit erratically, the men's lives improved and makeshift stoves – known as blowers – were made from the empty tins of food.

Eventually Mike was one of 20 more athletic-looking prisoners sent north to a new work camp near Bolzano in the South Tyrol. Here they were given extra rations to fuel them for work on a tunnel that would link the two great Axis powers via the Rome–Berlin Autostrada.

Here he laboured until September 1943 when his billet was peppered with automatic weapons fire as the Italians ran away south and the Germans came in from the north. Italy had capitulated.

The allied working party was now taken to the German province on Polish territory, of Upper Silesia.

A hint of desperation was discernible among the German guards of the Stalag, a discomfort that had not been evident in the Italian camps. Their new captors would organise random searches and this inspired a prank, reminiscent of the Colditz spirit, among the British prisoners, some of whom had been held captive since the Dunkirk evacuation in 1940.

'The psychology of the camp,' Mike told me, 'was that the French hoped they owned it, the Germans thought they owned it and the British knew they owned it.'

The innards of a radio and lengths of wire collected from the daily working parties, were twisted together and threaded along the ceiling of one hut, under the floor of the next, then along the ceiling of yet another. On the next snap search the bitter end was found by the German scrutineers and followed doggedly round the huts until it was traced to the dirt of the exercise yard where the prisoners were lined up waiting. At the end of the wire, a few inches beneath the ground was a buried Red Cross box with the catchphrase of the day written on it: 'You've had it, chums'. The snap searches were now increased – usually in the early hours of the morning – however as a punishment this was small beer compared with that meted out at a camp just a few miles from Mike's. No-one then had heard of Auschwitz. 'If we had of known then what the Germans were capable of we might not have been so cocky,' said Mike.

As German infrastructure was broken up by Allied bombing raids, so the Red Cross food parcels stopped getting through and the men started starving again.

Each night they were corralled into their huts by guards using unleashed Alsatians to round up any stragglers. The dogs were sleek, healthy and well fed. 'They enjoyed their work,' said Mike drily.

A trap was set for the conscientious hounds. Two men were dressed in extra battle dress with padding round the arms. Then a bunk-bed was taken apart and several men armed themselves with the stout corner posts. Round the back of their shuttered hut the dogs were easily lured, leaping at the waving arms of the padded prisoner. As their jaws sank into the padding, two of the dogs had a moment of disappointment before their skulls were stove in.

The whistles of their German masters did not bring the dogs back and the baffled guards' questions were answered the following day when their skins were found hanging from the perimeter wire. The carcasses had been cut up – there were butchers among the POWs – stewed and devoured by hungry men overnight. It was a defiant act.

But then again, no one had heard of Auschwitz.

Indeed the guards in charge of Mike's group, who had been sent to a sugar beet factory to work, were not fanatical SS men but broken down soldiers who had seen duty in 'Hitler's fridge', the Russian front. They were quite friendly and one prodded the collapsed end of his jackboot with his rifle butt to show Mike he had lost his toes from frostbite. One of the trucks of sugar beet that arrived for processing had a thin layer of the root vegetable covering the broken parts of a wrecked aeroplane. The captives sent it all through hoping it would damage the factory cutters. It was another act of defiance by the British POWs who were given favourable treatment compared to the Russians, and could take more liberties with their captors. When a poster went up in the camp entreating all Allied POWs to join with German forces to fight a common foe, the approaching Red Army, Mike and his colleagues went round heel clicking, and giving the Hitler salute, in classic masher-style mockery.

Behind their Stalag was an area of cleared pine forest used as a glider take-off and landing strip by the Hitler Youth organisation. It was a remnant of 1930s Germany, when Hitler – prevented from having an air force by the Versailles Treaty – set up 'flying clubs' instead for training purposes. One day Mike watched as two Hitler youth – no older than 15 – forced an elderly peasant woman to walk right around the perimeter of the airstrip rather than take a short cut across it. 'I remembered this later when I had a rifle in my hands once more,' said Mike.

Refugees from the east had started passing the camp and one day, during the bitter winter of 1945 when the temperature was 20°F below freezing the horse of a fleeing peasant dropped dead in front of the Stalag. The POWs were allowed to 'buy' it with cigarettes and 'ate like lords for a time'.

Shortly after this feast Mike and two other POWs were sent to a punishment laager on the outskirts of Dresden for being the slowest workers in the camp: they had been shovelling sand back onto a lorry that was supposed to have been discharging. Now they were put to hard labour in a quarry where dynamited rock had to be broken up with sledgehammers.

One day at about midday the workers became aware of the 'powerful drone of distant engines approaching'. This was followed by 'hundreds of undeviating vapour trails which had an arrogance about them'.

Mike watched as 4,500 tons of bombs were dropped on the helpless city: 'From the entrance to the quarry we could look down onto Dresden and I remember vividly when they unloaded their bombs that even the distant sound was such that I thought no one, but no one should be underneath that. We returned to the barracks in silence. We were all, prisoners and guards alike, stunned by what we had seen'.

When their punishment was finished Mike and his fellow POWs were led back to their Stalag through Dresden. 'When we'd arrived we'd passed through a pleasant city with horse-drawn traffic, we returned through a heap of rubble where the collapsed buildings tumbled down into the streets leaving a pathway only wide enough for a wheelbarrow to pass.' The Florence of the Elbe was no more. World War 2 had just 83 days left to run.

In a letter home, written later, Mike said: 'You will fry bacon and eggs, I'll have a drink with dad and then I want a holiday all on my own. I have never been on my own for four years and you would never believe how much I long for a bit of solitude "far from the haunts of men".'

Since the Bolzano work camp, Mike had befriended another soldier – Bob 'Bomber' Warnock, who boxed for his unit, the 31st Field Regiment, as a light heavyweight. The pair had been joined by Cap Barron, a South African, in the Stalag and this threesome had made plans to escape at the first opportunity. Their chance came unexpectedly one morning when a Soviet plane strafed a work party they were part of and the three plus another South African, Rosie Johnson, ran for their lives towards a nearby wood. The Germans soon came to their senses and started firing after them. Johnson was hit, and fell. The others never saw him again and ran on deep into the wood, confident the guards would not give chase but would instead cut their losses and take a firm hold of those left in the work party.

The trio pressed on ever eastward hoping to meet up with Russian forces, and came across two German corpses that they searched in vain for food and cigarettes. Cap left them and went his own way towards a hamlet desperate for a cigarette. He survived the war, Mike later learned.

Bomber and Mike were eventually picked up by two Russian soldiers on motorbikes, wielding carbines. They had learned enough Russian in captivity to be able to say 'I am an escaped English prisoner,' and were passed back through the line and given weapons.

Now part of the Red Army, the two former POWs turned west once more and started advancing through small hamlets until they came across a skirmish involving a German soldier on point duty to make contact with the enemy and who was shot dead by one of the Russians. Soon, tracer bullets set a barn alight where the rag-tag Soviet troops and their Allied assistants were searching for eggs. It was every man for himself and as Bomber and Mike ran for cover they threw away their carbines only moments before stumbling headlong into a German patrol who had rounded up their Soviet comrades. It was now time to explain they were POWs who had been picked up by the Russian patrol. This was readily accepted and they were prisoners once more in German hands.

They were held in a Luftwaffe prison: the only occupants as all the erring German airmen had now been seconded into infantry as the Germans fought a last ditch battle against the Soviets with anyone they could press into service.

Deep in this eerily empty jail, Mike and Bomber in adjacent cells used the German they'd learned to ask regularly after the health of the elderly soldier who brought them food. They worried he might be the only person who knew they were there. Should he die, they would starve to death.

Mike used a stub of pencil to make additions to the squadrons of Stukas, Focke-Wulfs, Messerschmitts and Heinkels that had been lovingly drawn on the walls of his cell. He added other aeroplanes flying in behind them: Spitfires.

'They were all technically accurate but after I'd finished, were steadily going down in flames. To help pass the time I tried to ration myself to one every hour.' Biggles eat your heart out!

Mike and Bomber's incarceration ended when they were taken to a nearby school where German troops were billeted and ordered to take a dog cart, laden with a soup urn, up to the front line every day.

Soon the school was shelled by Soviet artillery and, in the confusion, Bomber and Mike escaped again by walking out into the country only to be re-captured and handed over to a Volksturm unit made up of elderly veterans of World War 1. Their captor was a doddery old man with a bicycle and as he was almost sleepwalking through exhaustion the pair broke free yet again by jumping over a wall and hid in bushes overnight as Soviet troops over-ran the German positions. In the morning, with their one phrase of Russian, they were back in the Red Army once more, armed with carbines. They joined 12 other Allies in the multi-national force who were soon in action opening fire on Germans running away from a transport column which itself was under fire from a strafing Russian fighter plane.

From their position in a wood below the targeted road, they shot at the Germans, running for the shelter of the trees. 'I was a good shot,' said Mike, 'I aimed, squeezed the trigger and watched men fall.'

Taking shelter from mortar bombs, Mike leapt into a slit trench already occupied by a Russian soldier who seemed strangely unnerved by the explosions nearby. It was only when Mike noticed he had a fine coating of dust in his eye sockets he realised he was dead. 'It was the last place in the world you expected to see dust... on somebody's eyeballs,' he said.

Mike's war ended in Brux, part of the old German-populated Sudetenland area of Czechoslovakia which had been incorporated into Nazi Germany in 1938 according to the Munich Agreement. It was this agreement which British Prime Minister, Neville Chamberlain had 'negotiated' with Germany's dictator Adolf Hitler producing the much reviled 'Peace For Our Time' speech.

Fate had placed Mike in the crucible of World War 2 where he discovered that war had been over for two days. 'To get the knock during the war was one thing, now it was over was another thing entirely,' he said. The Soviets, who were fighting on against an SS unit in Brux, would not release any transport to them, although they did not stop Bomber and Mike commandeering a German troop transporter and driving off into American lines.

The veteran masher had survived.

• 5 •

Class Clash

Ａnd mashing he went. Mike and an old army pal Jimmy Barlow went on a drinking spree throughout the clubs and pubs of England financed with three years' back pay apiece. Wearing their 8th Army ribbons they were accepted wherever they roamed until Jimmy met a girl in Goole and so Mike went home to Radcliffe. 'My mother was relieved and pleased I'd come to my senses,' said Mike, who then packed up his hiking kit in preparation to go 'far from the haunts of men'. 'Where are you going?' his mother asked as *Over the Sea to Skye* was playing on the wireless. 'Skye,' came Mike's existential reply as the door slammed and he hit the road.

It took him a couple of days to hitchhike to Mallaig in Scotland where he arrived late in the day, missing the last ferry across to Skye. As the Highland dusk fell, Mike noticed a lonely barn that a farmer agreed to let him sleep in. The barn also sheltered a pregnant cow which was about to produce. The farmer, eager to have an undisturbed night, asked Mike to keep an eye on the heifer, only waking him up if anything happened. Mike explained that bovine midwifery was not in his range of skills to which the farmer answered: 'Don't worry, lad. If you see the beastie with a heed both ends, call me'.

For a fortnight Mike scrambled over the peaks of Skye's Cuillins re-adjusting to peace and emptying his mind of horror.

Back in Radcliffe, Mike hoped to re-train as an artist: he thought his eligibility for a government grant might be a little tenuous, as although his 'training' had been interrupted by the outbreak of war, it had amounted to no more than a couple of night classes a week.

Manchester Art School had been purpose-built in the heyday of industrial prosperity on the tram route out of town to the south. It was a vast black building in the Gothic style, with pointed cathedral windows. Its studios were in the Bohemian tradition, windowless, with vast skylights that let in the northern gloom to blandly light the life-model's room. Mike was to attend a selection board at the school and remembers feeling completely out of place among 'well spoken, well brought up, middle-class girls'. But he and several other ex-servicemen were accepted.

Mike noticed one of the 'middle class' girls struggling into the life-drawing room carrying her half-imperial board and box of pencils. She was slim and pretty with shoulder-length, wavy brown hair. Kathleen Herald was 16, the great niece of a famous painter, James Watterstone Herald.

She was appalled: the first day of her first term was spent among demobbed servicemen mostly in their late twenties, who had 'been torpedoed, imprisoned, blown up, shot down and, finally, kicked out'. They laughed, they swore; at lunchtime most of them got drunk. 'There must have been about 20 per cent of school-leavers, like me, amongst 80 per cent ex-servicemen.'

Kath was still an innocent Girl Guide at heart and had no way of ingratiating herself with these 'terrifying men'.

Very few of the ex-servicemen were plumping for pure art. They had a living to make and mostly went for commercial art, or illustration (now known as graphics).

The painters, of which Kath was one, joined the graphics horde for lectures on architecture and lessons in design and craft.

One afternoon Kath set off from the school to look for a museum where she had to study the history of textile design for homework. She wasn't sure of the way and asked someone who was walking up behind her.

'I'm going there myself. I'll show you,' he said.

She recognised him as one of the ex-soldiers in illustration, known as Mick. 'He was not my sort. He wasn't much of a conversationalist and we walked mostly in silence. He was stocky and brown and his hair had fallen out in large lumps that gave him a very odd appearance – one of the results, apparently, of having been a prisoner of war. He wore a mustard-coloured shirt which looked as if he had dyed it himself and an awful tie of mustard and maroon stripes which I later learned were the colours of the Northumberland Fusiliers. We parted in the Whitworth Museum to study our textiles. I copied minutely a French brocade which took me about an hour and a half.

'He, for the same exercise, submitted "The Polka Dot, a pattern which has stood the passage of time". I got A plus and he got C minus,' Kath recalled.

The girl who had grown up in Surbiton had met the miner's son who would become her husband. He was eight years older, with loose teeth and bald patches on his head from his POW diet.

'This Mick was said to be a bit of an oddball and a loner. He lived with his parents near Bury.' Kath had moved north with her family after her father, Joe, an engineer working in the water industry, had been promoted by his firm to be managing director of their works in Denton, Manchester.

The city's great Victorian public buildings were all black with engrained soot. Even its cathedral was black. There were no central parks or spaces, save bombsites, no trees, no squares, save miniscule ones. It was very different to Surbiton, it rained a lot. The only thing relieving her gloom were the carthorses pulling huge drays filled with bales of cotton which 'dipped their moustachioed lips into nosebags and stamped huge iron-shod hoofs at the flies'.

She started to explore the surrounding countryside, drawn by the distant horizon of Kinder Scout, and became addicted to rambling over the moors. She went on her own at weekends, with a map and compass and a packet of sandwiches, her skills as a Girl Guide coming into play. Over Kinder, down to Edale, up to William Clough to Snake pass and back down Doctors Gate to Glossop, she rambled over 'moors that stretched endlessly to the North which I thought I would never reach'. On warm days she would lie by a wall and listen 'to the streams burbling and the sheep calling and the grouse shouting "go-back, go-back, go-back".

'I felt happier then than I could ever remember. The loneliness and wildness of the moors was something I had never experienced before, cocooned in my London suburbs, aware only of the 'wildness' of Surrey. My first forays on Kinder opened up a new world to me, which was to provide the deepest satisfaction for a lifetime.'

Soon she heard that 'the oddball Mick' was in the habit of going off alone into the mountains and sleeping out.

'I had already noticed that he quite often appropriated my place at the window that faced the sunshine, and spent life-class rests leaning on the windowsill looking out, like me. He looked brown and hard, but I sensed already that he wasn't the sort of boy my mother would approve of. Not the sort to take home for tea'.

At a Valentine's Day dance, which Kath only reluctantly attended, she was asked for a twirl by the oddball.

'Like most ex-soldiers, he was a very good dancer. I didn't step on his feet, and found I was actually enjoying myself.' Later a group of six students all went to the pub where Mike saved Kath from embarrassment by saying, correctly, that she didn't drink. 'He got me a mineral water and deflected the amused scorn of his friends. I had never been in a pub before.'

After more dancing and talking, Kath decided she liked Mike. 'He also walked on the moors at weekends. I told him about my prancing across the tops, and a bond was forged.' Mike said he would take Kath back to the station to see her home.

They set off across the bombed wasteland towards Piccadilly. When they came to the canal crossing, he said, 'Are you hungry?'

'Yes,' Kath replied.

'We could have a meal down here,' said Mike who then climbed over the ironwork of the bridge and dropped down onto the towpath below. She followed. They walked along the canal side a little way, and then Mike stopped and pulled a tin of Heinz soup out of his jacket pocket. 'We'll cook this,' he said.

From another pocket he pulled out a tiny burner and a disc of paraffin wax. He punched holes in the top of the soup tin and wedged it on the little stove. 'We sat waiting for it to heat up. There was a distant hum of traffic above and beyond the high walls of the factories and warehouses that hedged the canal, but in our canyon it was very peaceful, with just the water lapping softly against the canal bank, and the stars reflected in the quiet surface.' The towpath snaked away round a curve and out of sight.

'It goes to Liverpool,' Mike said. Many years later they tried to return to this spot on a canal barge trip but were warned off it as teenage muggers were 'steaming' through barges: running their length stealing passengers' belongings.

'Drinking Heinz soup out of the tin beside the Manchester canal in the moonlight seemed to me infinitely glamorous. When I got home I didn't tell my mother what I had been doing, just that I had met a nice boy called Mick. I told her that he had been in the army all through the war. "Was he an officer?" she asked. "Yes," I lied.'

Every Wednesday, halfday at the art school, the couple walked up to the Town Hall to listen to the Midday Concert which was provided free by the Northern Orchestra under Charles Groves. After the concert they would go to a café in St Peter's Square or the Kardomah in Albert Square for a coffee and bun and then to a park to lie about and talk, or go rowing, or to look at the watercolours in the Whitworth Gallery, or to the pictures if there was a good film. Quite soon Mike suggested they should go walking together.

Their first bog-trot was to Holcombe moor, north of Manchester, bleaker than the Derbyshire moors, and closer to industrial works. 'But as we climbed up the side of the hill on the path that was half stream, half track, past the ancient stone walled farms with their yards full of sheep, I could hear the wonderful song of the curlew that haunted these northern uplands and the staccato warning of the disturbed grouse that had become pure music to my opened mind. It was like Finlandia again, discovering rapture, with the passion of the adolescent.'

In those days, before the Access to Mountains Bill was repealed, the moors were the preserve of the shooting classes and gamekeepers protected the grouse for their masters and saw to it that anyone trespassing was prosecuted. Kath always used the proper pathways over the moors, but Mike took no notice and bog-trotted where he fancied – even using the shooting butts for sleepovers! Once when he took Kath off the beaten track they were chased by a gamekeeper, but easily outran him as they were super-fit.

The 'nice Surrey estates and Crown woodlands in no way compared to these wild places I was now discovering'. Clothes rationing meant Kath only had a pair of school lace-ups, for hiking, but Mike took them to a cobbler's to get studs put in the soles. 'With studs I could then make that wonderful professional noise on the top deck of the bus when I got up from my seat and made for the stairs – hobnails on metal.'

But they did not help her keep up with Mike's pace. She would 'fall flat on my face in a bog or rick my ankle on a wall of rock'. But when she caught up there was a brew of tea in a billycan over the homemade stove. They cooked in an ex-army frying pan and Kath learned to wash pans with sand and gravel and use moss for a clean finish. 'Luckily my Girl Guide training had prepared me splendidly for all this, although with Mick we didn't waste time making mug hangers with forked twigs and string lashings. He never carried a tent, only a sleeping bag. I longed to sleep out, but knew I was already pressing my luck by coming home so late and smelling of wood smoke and falling asleep over supper.'

'Where do you go?' Kath's mother, Ivy, asked suspiciously. 'Who is this Mick?'

'He's my friend.'

'Perhaps you should ask him to tea,' said Ivy, whose idea of a suitable party was a public school boy with a sports car.

But Mike wasn't the cap-raising sort, the product of a nice school. He went his own way; he did his own thing, and he did not care a toss for anybody's disapproval. He did not say a lot, and had no small talk at all. He glared at people, and never made any effort to impress. He was a genuine hard case who had been attracted to Kath because she went bog-trotting on her own: 'Anyone who goes up there alone can't be all bad,' he told Kath nearly 60 years later.

'Before he came to tea with me, I went to tea with him, and the gulf was even greater than I had imagined,' she added.

Mike's home among the 'closely packed brick houses' had no bathroom and a communal lavatory in the back yard. When you went in at the door you were in the living room with a huge fire burning in the polished black grate. There was a sofa pulled across in front of the fire, a huge old sideboard against the wall, and a table against the inner wall, covered with a velour cloth. A velour curtain covered the way into the back kitchen and the yard behind. The sideboard bore an effigy of the Virgin Mary and there was an engraving of Jesus on the wall.

'Mick came from a Catholic family, although going to church was no longer a habit of his, nor of his father's. His mother was a slow-moving, stout lady of great kindness and lack of pretension.' They had been walking all afternoon and were tired and hungry, and on the table, straight out of the oven beside the fire, was a huge potato pie, awash with thick shin-beef gravy. Followed by tinned peaches and evaporated milk. 'It was fantastic. No fussing with manners and politeness, just hullo, eat this, you're welcome. And huge mugs of tea. It was the plainness that was so refreshing to me. There was no evidence that anything was especially for a visitor. I just felt I joined in what was normally there. My mother would have been steamed up all day about having a visitor.'

Mike in hiking boots, Kath still to get some

Emily's greatest fear about the 'prattling little girl' was that she might not be a Catholic.

After tea Mike escorted Kath to the station. It was dark and gas lamps were being lit by men with long poles as they walked along the cobbled streets. In the rain – the dampness had long been utilised by the mill owners to hold the spinning cotton together – the narrow streets shone, reflecting lights from the shops, and workers in clogs were coming home from the mills. 'It was like a scene out of Dickens and nothing like Surbiton at all,' said Kath.

Mike's sister Mary worked in a mill as a weaver and Kath realised it was a far harder thing for Mike to become an artist than it was for her, with her parents' backing and her famous great-uncle.

Mike told her: 'I am going to freelance when I finish. I'm never going to work in an office'. To that end he was determined to get into a London art school, just as it was Kath's ambition to get into the Royal College – never achieved by her, although the couple's daughter Hilary was more successful.

They both knew that whatever separated them was superficial. What drew them together was very real.

But the day Ivy returned Emily's hospitality and invited Mike to tea was a total disaster.

Joe contrived to be very busy under his car in the garage while Ivy set out the best china with its tiny teacups and fiddly trappings and, 'as was her want, talked nineteen to the dozen to cover up the fact that Mick said nothing at all'. Mike learnt all about his friend's childhood, about her writing – how she'd had a book published – about her famous artist great-uncle.

'I wanted to die and afterwards, when Mick had gone, she said I couldn't go out with him any more – he was too old, he was working class – what was I thinking of?! His accent! His missing lumps of hair! He wasn't my sort! She hadn't sacrificed herself to give me my brilliant education so that I could throw myself away on a man like that!'

Kath screamed at her. 'I said he had won the war for her, he was better by miles than all those namby-pamby public school boys she was always stuffing down my throat; he was real, he was honest, he was kind, he was more intelligent than anyone I had ever met, he had wonderful ideas, he loved the moors like me, he took me to art galleries and music concerts. His hair would grow back and one day he would have a car. I yelled and shrieked and cried, and my father stayed out in the garage examining the underneath of his Rover.'

Ivy had spent all her life bettering herself, climbing out of her working-class beginnings by sheer hard work: going to evening classes to learn secretarial skills, starting at fourteen on the lowest ladder as office dogsbody in Bill Morris's car factory and working her way up to become personal assistant to the boss in her department, Joe Herald. She married into a family who despised her as totally unsuitable for their dear only boy. She was beneath him, had left school at fourteen, and had a Birmingham accent. Her mother-in-law was bitter and cruel to her. Her own mother, who had died young of terrible gynaecological complications, had always told her she was 'the one we never wanted'. She had fought like a tiger all her life to better herself and, having done so, suffered from a grave inferiority complex now she mingled with the classes she had been so anxious to join.

'This is why it mattered to her so badly what the neighbours thought, why I had had to wear my good school uniform in public, why my boyfriend had to be respectable and suitable and presentable, not have a northern accent and alopecia.'

To see Kath – even Mike's shortening of her daughter's name from Kathleen was a repugnant working-class mannerism – throwing herself away was an unbearable disappointment to her.

'I love him!' Kath screamed.

'You don't know what love is!'

'It's you who doesn't know what love is! Look at you, you and Daddy! Is that what you call love? And he was old when you married him – forty! You're just a snob, a terrible snob! What's wrong with working class? It's more honest, it's more real, it's not all about manners. "Top dressing!"'

But, unwisely, Ivy had shown her hand. The more she disapproved of Mike, the more entrenched Kath became.

. 6 .

Design a Life

During the next summer art school break, Mike departed with his rucksack for Norway, and went hiking alone in the mountains, sleeping rough. He had been there before when he had met another hiker dressed eccentrically in dungarees with the arms and legs cut off and sandals. This was Sydney Chapman, assistant to Sir Frank Dyer of the Royal Greenwich Observatory who had a crater on the moon named after him. They travelled together, sleeping in the open, and one night Chapman woke Mike up to point out heavenly bodies to him. 'It meant nothing to me, then, the night sky, and he really opened my eyes to it,' recalls Mike, who many years later would check his tide table to ensure his passage would include a night sail when there was a full moon. On this second hitchhiking trip, in Oslo, he met a South African fireman, Brian Aldworth, ex-Royal Navy, who shared Mike's love of adventure. Brian lived in a rented room in London and offered Mike the sofa when he told him he was to continue his studies at the Central School of Art. Kath was left with another year at Manchester before she could try for London's Royal College of Art. 'The two of us found the parting very hard. After two years of friendship I had already found that, during the long intervals of college holidays when Mike went hitchhiking, I missed him terribly.'

Mike's digs on the top floor of a tall Georgian house in Bloomsbury were the proverbial artist's garret, and food was cooked on one gas ring atop the gas-fire. There was no bathroom, and just one 'dubious lavatory' two floors down. The students used the public bath-house in Holborn when they wanted a bath. The wallpaper was faded and very old, the bed a genuine Victorian brass bed, and the window glass was original, uneven and bubbly. Mike missed the great outdoors and would deliberately sleep rough in Green Park on warm summer nights just to keep his hand in; 'the sound of the passing traffic sounded like distant surf'. Mike's art lecturer had told his students not just to create objects d'art but to 'design a life' – a sentiment the war veteran took seriously.

Kath made occasional visits to London to see Mike. 'I thought it was incredibly romantic and craved to join this student life which seemed to me so much more authentic than in Manchester where most of the students lived at home, like me.' When they went out to eat in Charlotte Street they ordered one meal with two lots of utensils, which was the norm, sharing the table with a motley collection of down and outs. They would drink in the local, Black Horse pub, haunt of the literati and the intellectually renowned. By now Kath had progressed to shandy, 'three-quarters lemonade,' she recalled. 'Although I visited Mick alone in his room, nothing untoward took place, which might seem extraordinary now, but was quite normal at that time.' But a letter from Mike which included the phrase 'when you were sitting on the bed' was to fire up another row between Kath and Ivy. Kath kept Mike's letters tucked away in her underwear drawer.

'I came home one day to find my mother in a very strange mood. She looked as if she had been crying, and fidgeted about as if trying to bring herself to say something to me. Eventually she could contain herself no longer and burst out, "I read your letter. 'When you were sitting on the bed,' it said! What were you doing? What were you doing?" she screamed.'

'You read my letters!' Kath screamed back, outraged. 'How dare you read my letters!'

'I told you not to see him! I knew what would happen!'

'What do you mean – what would happen? What do you think happened? I was sitting on the bed because there aren't any chairs!'

'Sitting on the bed!' Ivy moaned.

'You have a beastly, filthy mind! Why can't I sit on a bed without you thinking...'

They were off again, hammer and tongs. The same old stuff. Ivy was ashamed of reading her daughter's letters, but couldn't stop her preoccupation with her unsuitable friend.

'Why didn't she leave me alone? I shall never know,' said Kath.

There were no mountains in London and on the weekends Kath did not come south, Mike went out on the River Thames: a new liquid adventure he'd discovered winding through the capital. Brian had bought a 12 ft canvas, double-seater, sailing canoe, *Vorlooper*, from a man he'd met in a Richmond pub. Mike and Brian explored the river as far west as Teddington where the saltwater ended. On one trip they paddled between a herd of cows standing knee deep in the river to cool off. Rationing was still a major part of their lives and here was a free fill up of milk, but *Vorlooper* was about as much use as a two-legged milking stool, and after a near capsize, the rustlers backed off. Anyway the appearance of the lock gates at Teddington suggested a river tamed, so the adventurers headed east instead.

Nights were spent sleeping aboard swim-headed Thames lighters – the marine equivalent of a barn – with the canoe tethered to their rusting steel sides. It took a while to get used to the clanging noise these great boxes made as they banged and rattled together from passing tugs' wash. A lighter's hold provided a perfect wind-break for firing up the Primus stove. The lighter roads were to be found in every reach and as the ebb died, the pair would simply clamber aboard the nearest to hand. One morning, pedestrians crossing Westminster Bridge were puzzled by the smell of frying bacon coming up from the river as Mike prepared breakfast beneath the shadow of Big Ben.

On Sunday evenings Mike and Brian would leave *Vorlooper* wherever the day ended them: a seascout HQ, sailing club or quiet back garden, until the following weekend when they returned. Boat repair was simple, when *Vorlooper*'s canvas hull needed patching, Mike would tear up an old handkerchief and dig out a gobbet of pitch from the seam of a nearby pill box, the World War 2 concrete gun emplacements which still straddle the sea-walls of the East Coast to this day. The tar was then heated up on a spoon over the Primus before being smeared over the rent receiving the patch.

In this way they explored the Thames in instalments learning hard lessons about tides and reefing: the canoe had a 12 ft mast and could be quite precarious in a breeze, until they got down as far as the sea.

Another student who shared Mike's digs was Peter Firmin, who went on to create TV characters including Basil Brush and Bagpuss. They also shared with a Jewish

Mike in his artist's garret

Peter Firmin helped create 'Bagpuss'

refugee from Germany, Eva Bernd, who was continually amazed by the freedoms enjoyed by her flatmates. 'You don't know what you've got,' she told them, although Mike had a good idea.

Peter was also loaned a canvas canoe from an old girlfriend who worked at Windsor Rep. It was a single-handed folding canoe and he asked Mike to help him paddle it down the Thames from the royal town. 'This was nearly my undoing. There was a small tear in the canvas so I tried repairing it with paint and a patch...stupid...it didn't last. There had been a lot of rain and the river was running high and fast. As we approached Richmond Bridge, me in the seat and Mike sitting behind, there was a sudden call from Mike: "Christ, Pete, we're sinking!" My first reaction was to get up and get out. Mike had a more sensible idea: "Sit down and paddle like hell," he called. So we did, heading for the bank and sinking all the while. Before we reached the bank the

Eva Bernd and Kath, bohemian babes

Mike in canoe: early paddling on the Thames

Brian Aldworth wanted to fight in Korea with Mike

water was up to my middle and the canoe sank and settled on a jetty which was flooded. We left it there and I returned later to do a proper repair.' Peter decided to adventure on land instead and when he told Mike he was off hitchhiking in France, the old soldier advised him: 'You need a really good down sleeping bag, a ground sheet, a billycan for tea and an enamel plate and cutlery including a sheath knife. Don't take a tent, sleep under the stars and hope to find shelter in bad weather.' Mike himself had been struck by the words of another art school colleague who told him: 'You can live off your memories as long as you keep making them'.

Some weekends Brian was on duty at Shoreditch Fire Station and Mike would return to *Vorlooper* alone. Once in Sea Reach, the last reach of the Thames before the open sea, Mike was paddling close to the legs of Southend Pier keeping out of the flood tide before heading across to the River Medway. Suddenly a Cockney mother's voice above him said: 'Don't spit, Alfie, you'll sink it'. Mike pretended he had not heard the detractor of his craft, and did not look up. Instead his face took on an appearance of fixed determination as he channelled his humiliation into paddling. Years later this would become an expression recognised by the readers of yachting journals the world over. The East End mum had provided Mike's 'eureka' moment. He had appeared in his own mental cartoon and the voice from above had provided the caption. From now on Mike would see the potential that boating provided for cartoons on just about every trip he made.

On Christmas Eve 1949, for instance, he was paddling alone on a new river: the Medway, which had endless creeks and marshes to explore, when dusk fell as he headed towards a handy barn in a fine drizzle. As he climbed out of *Vorlooper* he realised he had forgotten to pull the cockpit cover over his rations: two loaves of bread. He handed the soggy loaves to a pair of grateful piebald ponies, before laying out his sleeping bag in the barn. Once snug in the bag, doubts started to flood into his mind about *Vorlooper*'s security. Had he pulled her far enough up the marsh to be clear of the tide? Until he checked, there would be no sleep. Not wanting to pull on his wet but drying clothes again he scampered quickly back to the canoe in his underpants. The horses, expectant of more bread, trotted after him. A victim of absurdist circumstance, Mike had appeared in another cartoon, this one needing no caption.

The following summer Mike broke up a week before Kath and came home to Manchester. When they met, he asked Kath point blank to marry him.

'When?' she gasped.

'As soon as you're twenty-one, next week.'

'I shall be in llfracombe,' Kath said stupidly, referring to a family holiday already booked.

'If you say no, Brian and I are going to join up again and go to Korea. We've talked about it. We've both decided. But I said I'd ask you about getting married first.'

A brigade was being mobilised in England to go and fight in Korea following the Soviet-backed North Korean invasion of the American-backed South Korea in June 1950.

'But you can't!' Kath was aghast at the prospect.

'Marry me then. If you marry me, we'll go to the Alps,' Mike said, 'And live out until the winter comes.'

'What then?'

Mike just laughed. 'Who knows?'

It was not the sort of proposal Ivy would recognise and, not unexpectedly, she was furious.

'You can't marry him! He has nothing – nothing – to offer you! No money, no home. I know that sort! Where is your security? He will never get a job. He's a born wanderer. He'll wander off and leave you.'

But what he had offered was every bit as bewitching to the spirited young art student as a four-bedroom detached with en-suite bathroom.

Ivy said: 'Just see what your father has to say about it! This Mick of yours will have to come and see him, and tell us how he intends to keep you.'

The day was fixed and Joe had no stomach for the interview, but there was to be no more hiding under the car.

'I never asked Mick what he felt about it. He never talked about emotions or human relationships, or got excited, like me. He was in many ways just like my father – a man who got on with what he wanted to do without much bothering about other people and what they thought.'

Mike's directness had never been more naked during the meeting with Kath's father. Mike remembers it word for word to this day, probably because there's not much to commit to memory.

Joe: 'So you are thinking of getting married?'

'Yes.'

'When?'

'Saturday.'

'Oh...er, have you got a job?'

'No.'

'Are you thinking of getting one?'

'No.'

'Have you got any money?'

'Yes.'

'How much?'

'Forty quid.'

Even Joe had to laugh. He tried a compromise, and said they should get engaged and 'see how things go'. But Joe did not know about the real alternative: the adventure that beckoned in Korea.

Kath walked back to the London-bound train with Mike and he told her what had transpired.

'We shall be married next Saturday, else I'm going to Korea,' he said.

'But I'm going to Ilfracombe,' said Kath helplessly.

'I'll get a special licence,' said the war veteran, not sharing Kath's perception of a North Devon holiday resort as being an obstacle to the rest of their lives.

'I think, even at this stage, I might have backed off if my mother hadn't kept on and on saying how unsuitable Mike was and how could I possibly think of facing a homeless, moneyless future? On and on, non-stop,' recalls Kath.

So the young woman packed a case not just for a holiday but also for an elopement. In those days people could not get married under the age of 21 without parental consent. Kath's case included hiking boots, her stolen birth certificate, and her best dress – for the wedding itself. 'It was lucky we were going abroad, as I saw no prospect of being able to steal my ration book out of my mother's handbag,' she said.

The family set off for Ilfracombe in a distinctly non-holiday mood, William hating holidays as always, Ivy furious at her daughter and Kath preoccupied with how on earth she was going to get to London the following Friday without anyone noticing.

Then she got lucky: Kath was given a chalet annex in the garden of the family hotel all to herself and she'd noticed an enormous placard near the station with the times of the trains to London on it. There was an express at 8.30am. Breakfast was at 9. She would be well on her way to London before anyone found out she was missing.

The plan had included an arrangement to meet on Woking station in case Ivy called someone to meet the train in London and head off the errant pair. Changing trains would throw off any pursuers.

'I suffered the most terrible remorse at what I was doing to my parents who, in spite of all the evidence I have given to the contrary, I loved very dearly. They had been very good to me all my life. No child could have been happier from the day it was born,' Kath recalled.

She comforted herself in the knowledge that her brother Peter was getting married in the autumn and Ivy would have plenty of distractions. It didn't occur to her that the sole topic of conversation would be her elopement, and that the shame Ivy felt at her wicked behaviour would ruin even that day for her mother.

'"What people would say" had always been the yardstick of her life. I was providing enough material for tongue-wagging to last the century,' she said.

On the Thursday evening Kath wrote her farewell letter, which she propped up on her dressing table. 'It took me hours to write and I wept all the time I was writing it.'

Once the train was moving smoothly out of llfracombe station on its way to London, Kath forgot all the traumas which had made her 'engagement' such a misery and fell into a 'fever of excitement and happiness that increased with every mile I rushed through the glorious countryside'. She changed at Andover and got on a slow train to Woking arriving mid-afternoon. The door she was standing at came to a halt exactly opposite to where Mike was sitting on a bench.

I SUGGEST YOU AMAZE YOURSELF AGAIN AND GET IT OUT,
THIS TIDE IS RISING

'He got up and came towards me, and didn't say anything. Neither did I. As the train was still standing there we got back on it and went to London.'

The night before the wedding, Mike had arranged for Kath to spend the night in the care of an Irish girl called Kitty.

The following morning in her best dress Kath went to meet Mike but hardly recognised him. 'Instead of his usual old cords and shirt he was wearing his navy-blue double-breasted demob suit, still creased out of its box. He looked ghastly.'

She told him: 'I can't marry you looking like that!' 'It's awful!'

'What's wrong with it?"

'It doesn't look like you! Go and put your ordinary clothes on!'

Having changed into his Mike clothes the pair walked up Southampton Row to the registry office, with Kitty, Kath's hostess of the night before.

Kitty said, 'Have you got the ring or has Brian got it?'

'The ring!'

Material symbols of unity meant little to this couple who had hiked together through fair weather and foul, darkness and daylight for hundreds of miles over the moors and peaks around Manchester. They trusted each other implicitly. They had the highest respect for each other. They were two of a kind, bonded in their own estimation, yet polarised by a superficial social spectrum. Neither had given 'the ring' a second thought. Five pounds raised between them, a nearby jeweller with a tray of second-hand rings and convention was served. Many years later Kath lost the ring while choosing vegetables in a local greengrocer.

'And when is the happy event to take place?' said the shopkeeper.

Left to right, Brian Aldworth (best man), Kath Peyton, Mike Peyton, wedding day after elopement

Mike looked at his watch, 'In five minutes'.

At 11am with Brian Aldworth as best man and Kitty and two students as witnesses, Mike and Kath were married at the Russell Square registry office. The female registrar sensed she was witnessing a union in need only of administrational advice and said to Kath, 'Don't forget to get your name changed on your ration book'.

A student friend had a wedding cake made in a small café dubbed the Waffle Brothel in posh but seedy Bayswater, which the guests consumed with fizzy wine before repairing to the cinema to see the Marx Brothers in *A Day at the Races*.

Kath's wedding gifts included a pair of walking boots, a sleeping bag and the offer of *Vorlooper* as a honeymoon cruise ship lying at Stoke on the River Medway behind a marshy delta of creeks. Mike's included a gift from Sydney Chapman: a book about self-sufficiency and simple living called *Walden* by the American philosopher Henry David Thoreau. 'It had a great influence on me,' Mike, said, although he would never be a disciple of any creed but his own. As a stubborn individualist, he had long been drawn to the attractions of asceticism, especially having seen what sacrifices chasing small luxuries entailed in England's industrial heartland. He was simply stunned that someone had formalised his experience into a philosophy. It was a 'why didn't I think of that?' moment.

The honeymoon would start by sailing and paddling *Vorlooper* up the Medway, before making for Dover and the Channel crossing to the Alps.

The newlyweds spent the first night of their honeymoon in sleeping bags below the sea wall, with their hiking boots as pillows.

'I looked up at the stars and thought myself the happiest woman in the world. The canoe was pulled up on the shore, the tide receding across the mud, and the wading birds on the waterline were silhouetted against the lights of Chatham twinkling far away on the other side. Distant noises of a tug hooting, the soft diesel throb of a cargo ship out beyond the Nore, mingled with the nearer warbling and trilling of the birds. The grass was cold and smelled of the sea. I lay and looked up at the sharp September stars and thought of all the things that were going to happen. I knew it would all be, in spite of what my mother had said, quite marvellous,' Kath wrote in her diary.

They ventured on up the Medway and at Aylesford Lock at dusk in the gently falling rain they were offered the fo'c'sle of the sailing barge *Lancashire* for the night, where they slept wrapped up in a spare staysail. Her skipper, Tubby Blake,

Kath prepares a honeymoon dinner

Kath with honeymoon canoe. On the Ouze near Newton Blossomville, August 1954

Mike paddling up the River Medway

sailed with his wife as mate and sympathised with Kath's plight. As it turned out it was to be one of their more luxurious overnights.

At Tonbridge they left *Vorlooper* with a sea scout school, whose troop leader introduced himself as Major General Jenkins, 'but you can call me Blue Eagle', and hitchhiked to Dover. The rest of their adventurous honeymoon was spent sleeping rough: under bridges, in barns, bus shelters, even on one occasion inside a large drainpipe! In Paris they spent a week in an attic on the Rue St Denis. In Cannes a cave served them well, in Villefranche a disused fountain and, having crossed the Alps, they enjoyed the luxury of youth hostels until reaching Pisa where thanks to the Vatican pronouncing a new holy dogma, Mike rediscovered his Catholicism and, as a pilgrim, spent the night in a monastery while Kath slept in a convent. The pair also visited Lourdes and were a little chastened to see pilgrims drinking the holy water which ran down from the Pyrenees as just the night before while sleeping rough they had used the stream for freshening up.

The £40 lasted them three months in which time they visited Florence, Venice and the Tyrol.

There was a shortage of many commodities after the war and pocket money could be made by collecting waste paper: old newspapers, obsolete telephone directories, cardboard boxes for re-cycling. It was known as salvage.

'I still reckon that I am the only bride that ever had to collect salvage in Paris to earn her fare back across the Channel,' Kath recalled.

Kath and Mike in the Alps

• 7 •

Marsh Country

Grey smoke drifted up through a spinney of dead winter trees alerting me to the hidden chimneys of Rookery Cottage, the Peytons' home, which stands lonely and isolated in fields near the River Crouch in Essex. Behind the cottage, grey lag geese dropped down from a featureless grey sky and skidded across ice on a large pond. Inside I sat by an open fire fuelled by poplar logs from trees blown down in Kath's Wood, which the pair have spent many years planting.

Two replica Aldo Casanova stone lions lay asleep on each side of the hearth, while in front of me cringed Jacko, the mongrel dog rescued after its skull was fractured in the jaws of a Rottweiller. Mike stood warming himself in front of the fire as Kath searched through their vinyl record collection against the book-lined room.

'Good God, even a charity shop wouldn't take these records, they're so old,' she said, '…like us I suppose,' and then found what she was looking for. She placed a warped disc on the turntable that crackled round and round until a ghostly cry was emitted from the speakers. It echoed round the room. It was the call of loons, or great northern divers, birds which at night had been their only company while sleeping rough in the Canadian Lakes.

As Kath explained the high-pitched, eerie call, Mike's mind was elsewhere he had, unnoticed by his wife of nearly 60 years, removed a large copper clock from the chimney breast and turned the hands round. 'What time did you say dinner was?' he asked.

'Old greedy, always thinking of your stomach,' said Kath, 'eight o'clock,' she added. That there was nothing wrong with Mike's memory was evident from the clock which he now alerted Kath's attention to.

'Yes, all right, it's nearly ready, I suppose you'd rather listen to that awful dirge of Bob Roberts…' and then turning to me, 'he likes Leonard Cohen, too,' she said with incredulity, 'can you imagine listening to that? I prefer Brahms…or Elvis,' she added, as the loons stopped their other-worldly cry.

After graduating from Manchester School of Art, Kath was employed as a teacher at the Northampton High School. Mike worked for a while in a toffee factory, but he was determined to make a success of drawing cartoons, so from the cottage they rented in the village of Weedon, near Daventry, which was beside the A5, he hitch-hiked down to London to go through the back-numbers of magazines to get ideas for cartoons he thought he could supply. He would work his way around the capital visiting the *British Legion Journal*, *Scout* magazine, *Headlight*, *Modern Caravan* and *Commercial Motor* among others. He also invented a strip cartoon for *Swift* comic: Mono the Moon Man, about an inhabitant of the Moon who came down to Earth. 'Sometimes they'd suggest ideas themselves,' said Mike, 'although the editor of *Scout* told me I was the "scoutiest non-scout" he'd ever met.' Mike's travels to London were

Camping in the Canadian outback

so frequent he became known to local lorry-drivers who would turn up outside the cottage and sound the horn. If Mike was going south he would flash the house lights on and off to let the driver know he'd soon be with him.

Kath was now keen to settle down and start a family, but Mike suggested they had one more adventure before committing themselves to children. They hit upon hiking and canoeing in Canada, a land of lakes and mountains, and started saving seriously.

'When we'd got enough money to go to Canada I sent Mono back to the Moon,' Mike told me over dinner.

'Well, bring him back again,' said Kath, 'we could do with some more'.

In April 1955 they paid £60 each for a one way ticket by sea to Montreal aboard a ship on her last voyage, the *Empress of France*. The weather was very rough, all the furniture was chained down and 'often I'd be the only one at table,' said Mike.

'Old piggy there,' added Kath.

They got jobs in service in a large house in Toronto where Kath cleaned and looked after the babies and Mike worked as a freelance graphic artist, even designing labels for packs of sausages. The mistress of the house, a Hungarian immigrant, was a little parsimonious and Mike and Kath were obliged to eat the leftovers, 'even the children's,' Kath recalled. They also took evening jobs, as the city was not where they intended to stay: they were saving for exploration in the great outdoors. Mike worked in a bowling alley, which had its risks as he had to run two alleys at the same time and when vaulting from one to the other: 'you would often arrive at the same time as a strike with skittles flying in orbit'. They both also worked as worm pickers on a golf course. This entailed walking the links during the hours of darkness with two cans strapped on their legs. One was full of sawdust to make it easier to pick up their prey; the other was the receptacle. They had lights on their heads that also alerted the worms to their fate so they had to be quick. They sold them by the hundred and on a 'moist night it could be a profitable occupation'.

After three months' work they had saved enough for their travels. They bought a Morris Minor and Mike was asked where he had learned to drive. 'In the Western Desert,' came his droll reply. From Toronto Library Mike had discovered that the old time trappers lived off what was known as the three 'b's – bacon, beans and bannock, a dough made from flour and water. So with an ample supply of trapper grub they drove 300 miles north in Ontario where they hired a canoe and set off for a voyage through lakes and forests with names marked on the map such as Expectation, Desperation and Salvation lakes. 'It was terrifying really, we saw no living soul for days,' said Kath.

There were times when they had to carry the canoe overland between lakes. Such portage could be up to two miles long. The 70 lb canoe Mike carried over his head. 'You were scared stiff of slipping,' said Mike, 'and damaging the canoe because you could never have got out through the forest'. The forests were so dense that the dead trees couldn't fall down.

At night they camped on islands, to minimise the fire risk from cooking, and listened to the call of the afore-mentioned great northern diver, which echoed through the forests and across the dark surface of the lakes. 'It seemed to sum up the very essence of the Canadian Lakes and we knew we were the only people hearing it. As the poet

Canoe portage during the Canada trip

put it, a hundred thousand miles from all the wheels that run,' said Mike. Their only luxury was a spoonful of Golden Syrup dabbed on a bannock, which they allowed themselves at the end of a hard day's travelling. One day they came round a bend in a narrow channel and came face to face with a moose. They had been told the beasts could charge. 'But fortunately he was the one who panicked, not us, and went the other way,' said Mike.

Back in civilisation they crossed Canada on the dirt road that would become the Trans Canada Highway. It was virtually unused as travellers crossing the country drove south to use the American highways with their gas stations and eateries. They took off into the Rockies, this time on foot. The trip was limited by the amount they could carry over wild and rugged country. At one time they were crossing a river that was too deep for comfort and it was raining heavily. The flow was so strong they had to cut poles from mature saplings to lean on, planting them upstream and crossing the river in a series of semi-circles. Once ashore a few slashes with the hand axe provided some dry pine and in minutes they had a fire going and with their well-practised drill a shelter was erected, beneath which they dried out. When the food had almost run out they sat on the Great Divide to decide whether they should go west and work in Vancouver or head east to New York and get a boat back to Britain. But Canada, like America, was too materialistic for their tastes. One incident had summed up both countries for the intrepid duo. In Dakota while supping coffee in a diner, a driver came in and, addressing the occupants in general, said: 'There's been a bad accident down the road – a this year's model Cadillac smashed to hell!'

With the year-long trip over and the wanderlust sated, at least temporarily, Mike and Kath returned to England. Kath was by now making a living from writing children's novels. Mike helped with the plotlines and she wrote under the name K M Peyton. The M stood for Mike she revealed many years later to Mark Lawson on BBC Radio 4's *Front Row* programme on which she was interviewed to celebrate the approach of her 80th birthday. But they were to lead to more 'serious writing' bringing her continued success and a string of awards. In those early days Kath also wrote 'far-fetched serials for girl's comics' and was so prolific she soon gave up her teaching job. Mike supplemented his freelance work by cleaning out pubs. They never refused work, whatever was offered, and it ranged from painting a hundred biscuit tins by hand for the Medici gallery to designing a poster exhorting a South African coal-miner to keep his tin hat on at work. They had their thin periods, but were avid savers, and could exist for months at a time on stewed mutton and rice if the goal were tempting enough.

They had moved to London because of Mike's work drawing cartoons where they kept in touch with their old art school friends, Joan and Peter Firmin. Peter recalls how at the digs he and Mike once shared, a window got broken during a party. They enlisted the help of a student, Peter White, who was studying stained glass at the Central School of Art. Mike produced a legend to go with the window – of a man with eyes looking through the hair on the back of his head – 'Good friends, good books, an easy conscience and eyes in the back of your head'.

The Peytons lived in rented accommodation in Camden Town and after their adventures in the great outdoors were not enjoying being such urban creatures. So they drew a circle with a 50 mile radius around London – the place where Mike's work was – to see what countryside it encompassed. By now they both shared a deep love of mountains, but alas there were no such features in the topography of the Home Counties. Instead there was the river. The Upper Reaches of the Thames – those close to London anyway – were too manicured for their pioneering tastes. So they turned east. They looked at property along the banks of the scene of their honeymoon, the River Medway. But away from the marsh everything appeared to be covered in grey dust of cement in those days. The man who would become Britain's last sailing barge skipper, Bob Roberts – whose sea shanties Mike enjoyed and Kath loathed – remarked on what he described as 'cementism' in his book *Coasting Bargemaster*. 'One of the most beautiful parts of Kent overlooking the lower reaches of the river has been desecrated by the white dust from the tall chimneys of several huge cement works which are clustered in the district. For nearly 10 miles the rooftops, trees, bushes – everything – are laden with this repulsive coating... apparently there was no law to stop the polluting of great areas of lovely scenery and possibly the injuring of the health of thousands of men, women and children who daily breathed this awful atmosphere.'

That only left Essex.

They had never set foot in the county before but came out of London with a list of estate agents' houses to look at, starting in Maldon. They had a thousand pounds in cash, so the range could be called limited, and there was no chance of a mortgage for they were self-employed and self-employed people couldn't obtain mortgages then.

The properties all sounded dull in the extreme, especially the 'pebble-dashed semi near station in South Woodham Ferrers, £800'. But this was the only one left on the list, once they'd ruled out two in Maldon – a town they immediately took to.

It was February and snowing softly, and not the best time for viewing, but as they returned to Maldon bus station in the late afternoon, they saw a bus just about to

Clements Green Creek, Mike's first sailing station

depart with South Woodham on its board. Remembering the pebble-dashed semi they ran and leapt aboard as it pulled out.

'Two to South Woodham please.'

They had no idea how far it was, so after some miles they asked the conductor. The pebble-dashed semi's address was Clements Green Lane.

'Do you know where Clements Green Lane is?' Mike asked.

'No, but that's Clements Green Creek,' the man said, and gestured out of the window. The bus was just coming over the brow of a hill and below them in the fast-closing dusk they saw a river valley with a creek winding off the main river, snaking towards the bottom of the hill where shone the lights of a small farmhouse. In the last, weak, pinkish light from a dying sun they had a momentary view of a very different kind of wilderness than that they were used to. But they were drawn to it. There was no sign of town or noisy transport or proximity to London, just an empty valley of marsh with skeins of geese crossing the darkening sky.

'Our optimism rose and excitement took over,' said Kath, 'The bus stopped at the station but there was no one there. A handful of station houses, a shed that sold newspapers and sweets which was closed'. They walked down a lane shrouded by high elms going towards where they thought the river must be. A dun horse grazed, lifting its head incuriously as they passed. The lane was just mud and potholes surrounded by fields, the odd house here and there and a tin church. As they continued down the lane a snipe flew up under their feet.

'This is perfect,' said Kath, 'whatever the house is like – this is wonderful'.

It was deep, unspoilt country with a smell of the sea and the distant warbling of waders on the tide line. There were no lampposts, no pavements, no sops to suburban living. There was a bend in the lane to the left, another pond on the right, and a drive going up beside it to a little house huddling in the darkness – the house they had come to see. Even as they walked up the drive they knew they were going to buy it, whatever it was like.

Its windows were broken and it was covered in ivy. Outside the back door was a pile of old Camp coffee bottles. There was a lean-to kitchen there, at the back a glass conservatory with what appeared to be a vine in it, and on the far side a door with a porthole in it that looked into a bathroom. The back wall had fallen out and the bath was open to the sky.

'Oh, I love this,' said Kath. 'A vine!'

They peered through the French windows that opened into the conservatory and could make out just one room, with narrow wooden stairs going off up a right-hand wall. That was all they could see in the gloaming.

The cottage was set in an acre of ground, a long narrow acre like all the other old plot land houses of the district. They were like houses built on allotments. The semi next door was quiet. A hedge divided the two, and there was an orchard with turkeys in a shed. Their patch had a hedge across it beyond a small back lawn supporting a couple of apple trees, with a barn, and fields beyond.

Back at the station, which advertised three trains to London a day, they gathered in the waiting room which had a coal fire burning and a pile of magazines to read on the table.

'We had found a phone box and rung the agent and told him we definitely wanted the house and he mumbled something about somebody else having a survey done. We said we didn't care about a survey, just take the money. He said he would ring us in the morning.'

'Of course, everyone thought we were mad.'

By now Kath was two months' pregnant and was keen to get her house organised. One Sunday they got the keys off the agent to look at their new home in daylight. They took the train accompanied by the Firmins and their two-year-old daughter Charlotte. Joan Firmin was eight months' pregnant with the couple's second child and so the two women offered each other support. Being Sunday there were no trains farther than Wickford, but they caught a bus to Southend which they were told would take them halfway. The rest they would have to walk.

'There was hardly any traffic, as I remember us all walking in the middle of the road, taking it in turns after a mile or so to carry Charlotte. We were such urban creatures that a Sunday morning in such remote country was a treat,' Kath said.

Their new home was called Greenlands, which they later changed to Long Acre. 'I must admit it looked forlorn,' said Kath.

The old clapboard kitchen sagged dangerously, the broken windows stared, all the floorboards in the downstairs room were rotten and falling through. The bedroom windows looked out over next door's turkeys, and the roofs of the scattered houses – mostly shacks – farther down the lane. Most of South Woodham Ferrers looked like an old North American gold-rush shanty town with wooden sheds, old railway carriages, even an upturned boat all serving as homes. But the precious metal in this case was the two gleaming steel lines which had brought the railway in 1925 and so cheap housing for Londoners. The original Woodham Ferrers, pre-railway, was at the top of the hill, with its ancient church, old pub and ancient cottages – much older than the shacks of its lowland twin. South Woodham in 1956 was a motley collection of shacks and railway carriages scattered around some mud lanes. The only tarmac was on the Wickford–Burnham road and on the Hullbridge road which went straight down to the river. All the other roads, in spite of their elegant names – King Edwards Road, Victoria Road, Albert Road, Clements Green Lane – were just mud and pot-holes where about 300 residents shopped at sheds that sold anything from paraffin to henfood, knitting wool and shoes. There was a post office, now a One-Stop, a primary school, Elmwood. There was a tin Church of England and a tin Evangelical church, a Village Hall and a station. 'Percentagewise there were more shops to serve three hundred people then than there are today to serve 20,000,' said Kath.

'But we knew nothing of what South Woodham would become,' she added, 'We ate our sandwiches sitting on the best of the floorboards and made our plans. With £200 left after the purchase price we thought we would have enough to put the floor and

The marshes at Woodham. When Mike and Kath first moved here, houses had bungs in the floorboards to release water after big tides

The River Crouch, its historic reaches beguiled Mike

windows right, mend the bathroom and put in a hot water system. The rest would have to wait, apart from buying a stove for the kitchen. The only thing in the kitchen was an old stone butler's sink and a cold tap. The place was technically uninhabitable.'

They returned with a hired van carrying all their wordly goods: an army double bunk (no mattresses), two sleeping bags, a bicycle, two tin trunks of clothes, kitchen items and trade tools. The Cockney driver, pulling up outside the house on a perfect June day, sat looking out on the hip-high grass, the nettles round the house and the great swags of hanging ivy swinging across the broken glass and said, 'Rather you than me, mate'.

With planks laid across the broken floorboards, a table made from two oil drums and an old door, and a fire in the grate from wood picked up around the garden, they moved in. In the morning Kath was frying bacon and eggs over the open hearth when there was a knock on the back door. 'Although on all our wanderings in mountains and abroad we had always cooked on an open fire, and never carried either a tent or a primus, to cook on an open fire in a house struck me as unaccountably sordid.

'I looked up to see John Coward the milkman peering in, rather hesitantly. His cart with a horse in the shafts was parked at the bottom of the drive,' she said.

'Would you like milk delivered?' he asked.

'Oh yes please', said Kath nonchalantly.

He produced two pints and departed.

Their sleeping bags spread across the bare, mattress-less bunk beds were not as inviting as they once had been in the lee of a rock on a windy hillside. Their climbing boots were hung up over a rafter in the loft, gathering dust.

In those days there was a market at Wickford every Monday which sold high-quality fabrics, ends of rolls from London, from which Kath made all her own clothes and later the children's.

She was looking forward to getting the place sorted with that spare £200, but she hadn't reckoned on Mike's first boat.

· 8 ·

A Rise-on

Their muddy lane, bordered with blackthorn hedge, meandered down to the sea wall on the other side of which Mike was discovering another kind of bog-trotting, a bogginess of salt water. As he explored the marshes, covered in mauve-tinted sea lavender, and brittle grass, which flanked the River Crouch, he started to sense a new kind of canvas: the vast, unrestricted skies of the Essex flatlands. Here the only mountains available were of white cumulous clouds blowing sedately across the vivid blue sky of summer. Larks twittered high over sea walls which snaked away each side of creeks for mile upon mile towards – somewhere far in the hazy distance – the open sea. Mike, who rarely ever wore a wrist-watch, was thrilled by the water-clock provided by the tides, which had ebbed and flowed since time began: 'the pulse-beat of eternity' as the late Essex historian Hervey Benham put it. Across on the opposite bank of the river, Mike learned that the ridge, which blanketed the south-west wind, was the crest where the future of England was decided in 1016. Here Dane met Saxon and Saxon lost, putting King Canute on the throne. This was truly a great outdoors and one on the doorstep which Kath was cleaning.

'After we had been there two or three days Mike said to me, "Come for a walk. I've got something to show you."'

It was a lovely sunny evening, not a cloud in the sky. They set off down the lane away from the village, past the few motley small-holdings that straggled to the end. The lane turned and climbed uphill, but Mike continued straight on along a track that followed a ditch full of feathery reeds and the twittering of reed-warblers. A curlew cried, reminding them of moors and mountains, but ahead lay just a flat horizon. Then the path made a sudden foray up a bank.

'I ran up and nearly fell headfirst into the river, brimming at my feet. It was such a shock that I shouted out. "Clements Green Creek!" I had forgotten all about it in my homemaking, and now found we had this lovely stretch of water barely five minutes walk from our front gate. Mike had purposely chosen the timing for the tide was right up, the water lapping the top of the wall that kept it out of the fields.'

The creek had once been used by a nearby farm, to export its crops on sailing barges.

'The creek was wonderful, glittering in the evening sun, the empty marshes stretching away beyond as far as the eye could see. Farther down some children were swimming,' Kath recalled.

'We could keep a boat here,' Mike said quietly, as he chewed on a blade of grass, lying on his back. With timing like that he needed no watch.

They walked along the sea wall, downstream, and came to a bungalow built beside the water. There was a kink in the wall with a diving-board rigged out over the creek. Other wooden houses included one with barns that belonged to Peter Pointer, a shipwright and bird-fancier.

'This was all strange country to us then, but the creek soon became our home as much as our own garden. We swam there at high water and so did many of the village people, including the midwife and the doctor. To lie on one's back in the creek on a summer's day listening to the skylarks singing was as near to perfect peace as one can find in this world,' Kath said.

'Of course we all know that the tide goes down as well as comes up and the Essex rivers look quite different when banks of mud shine in the rain,' she added, her knowing but characteristically sardonic smile playing across her face. It doesn't do to show too much romantic dottiness.

Much of Woodham is below sea-level and before the builders drained it and made the sluices, for which residents were charged 'sea-drainage rates', sea water regularly flooded many homes in the village. At high tide in the winter when there was a lot of rainwater, Clements Green Lane would flood up to Long Acre and the Peytons could only access their home in Wellington boots. At the railway station commuters would leave their wellies upside down on the spikes of the iron fence ready to be picked up in the evening.

Though their house was never actually flooded, on big tides the water lapped at the kitchen door. They have photos of the children rowing the dinghy on the front lawn and Kath has a vivid memory of a small child one wet summer, stark naked save for her gumboots striding down the lane waving a Union Jack.

For fresh eggs the Peytons kept four chickens: Matthew, Mark, Luke and John, which Mike fed by hurling grain out of the upstairs window. By now he had commissions to draw cartoons for the *The New Scientist*, under editor Percy Cudlipp, of the famous newspaper family, and also on *The Spectator*, which entailed spending a day with each at their respective London offices. This was inconvenient as it meant Mike had to buy a suit. Kath found him a nice tweed two-piece and was very proud of her smartly dressed husband getting the train to work like other bread-winners, at least on one day a week. Kath spent the mornings writing 'teenage novels'.

In 1956 Mike's father Jeremiah, died of cancer. Mary told him he had spent his last days on morphine that had the disturbing effect of bringing back the horrors of the trenches. He would sit by the window brushing imaginary rats off his lap.

In November that year Kath went into labour. They rang for the ambulance at four on a Sunday morning, but Mike made it wait while he made a bag of bacon sandwiches, for there were no buses on a Sunday and he would have to hitchhike home from Chelmsford Hospital. He offered Kath a sandwich in the ambulance but she declined as she felt carsick.

'Husbands – thank God – didn't stay with their wives to witness the birth in those days so I was left alone to get on with it, and Hilary was born in the evening.' Her name satisfied Mike's mother as Hilary was the name of a saint – albeit a male one – but also the name of a joint hero of her parents: Sir Edmund Hillary, the Everest mountaineer. Many years later Mike and Kath were invited to lunch at the House of Lords by John Hunt who organised Hillary's climb. He had read Mike's article for the *Geographical Magazine* on their own 177 kilometre hike and climb across the peaks of Corsica.

Mike visited his wife and new baby by bus the following morning, bringing large bunches of grapes off their own vine which the other mothers thought very extravagant. Kath didn't tell them they were free.

Fortunately Long Acre had by then a hot water system in place although the kitchen was still a ruin. It had a cooker and the old stone butler's sink, but nothing else, although a plug-in boiler was donated for washing the nappies, which was a Godsend for Kath.

Their GP was old Doctor Frew from Wickford, who visited the village twice a week. He held a surgery in the parlour of one of the railway cottages.

Their second daughter was born at home 15 months later, delivered by a midwife.

She, too, was named to please Emily's religious beliefs. Saint Veronica accompanied Christ to Calvary, but she was also the name of Everard's race winning Thames sailing barge! 'It could have been worse,' Veronica told me half a century later, 'I could have been called Speedwell!'

During all this baby-rearing time Mike was anxious to start sailing. In the summer after Hilary's birth they decided to charter a boat for a fortnight and see how they got on. Mike went off on his bicycle looking at charter boats in Maldon and Heybridge and, later, one at Hayes farm, the caravan site on the road to Wickford. On his return from this journey he was even more introspective than normal. He said, after continued probing, that the boat was very nice, a 24 ft, centre-board, gunter-rigged sloop known as a 'penny sick' as she had formerly taken people for trips off Southend Pier.

'How much does it cost for a fortnight?' asked Kath.

Silence.

'Well, how much?'

'Quite a lot. I bought it.'

The penny sick had cost the £200 (less a fiver as the owner took pity once he realised it was everything the couple had) earmarked for the kitchen, and Mike's selfishness was not well received.

Vagrant

'He made a feeble joke about my being the only woman in Essex with a gaff-rigged kitchen but I wasn't amused', said Kath.

The boat, christened *Vagrant*, was moored in Clements Green Creek. She was not alone there, Peter Pointer over the sea wall being an able shipwright. Other odd craft lay about – none were of the thoroughbred Burnham ilk – and the bare ribs of discarded smacks appeared at low water, as they did everywhere down the river. Hammering echoed across the mud, mixing with the cries of Peter's peacocks. Peter was a spare, wiry figure with a dark beard and gipsy eyes, who had once sailed on one of Erikson's square-riggers from London to Cardiff. An ex-glider pilot with the Parachute Regiment, he had returned home on demob to find his wife in bed with another man. The story went that he walked out without a word and soon afterwards found his natural home on the side of the creek. He built his own house and all the sheds that housed his collection of wounded owls, winged seagulls and battered ducks. Living there with him was the village schoolmistress, a splendid old-fashioned teacher called Marion Hicks who demanded, and got, the best out of the 60 children in the school.

The men who had boats in the creek included Frank Pynn, an ex-naval signaller who sailed an old Broads boat, and Tom Bolton who owned the smack *Maria* CK 21 and sailed everywhere with his mongrel dog. The smack had cost him £10 but he recouped his money by selling the eels he caught in her bilges. There was a home-built barge yacht, *Marie*, whose owner joked that she was so poor to windward that a drifting mattress had beaten him down the river 'cos it had got a better slant!' All these characters clubbed together and bought an old wooden lighter, *Lillian*, and beached her on the saltings to use as a dry dock. They also built a grid just upstream with high posts to make a boat fast to, so that bottoms could be scrubbed and topsides painted. The blackened bones of *Lillian* and the weed-covered grid are still there.

It was a lively spot, and the Peytons loved going down there along their 'grassy path'. When there was a village competition for a collection of wild flowers, their children won with a vase of 52 different varieties, all picked on the grassy path. The

'...realised the gulls were standing not floating'

"AND SHE HAS A FULL SUIT OF STORM CANVAS, SEA ANCHOR…"

children knew the names of all of them. They also knew not to pick orchids – which also grew wild then. It was a micro-world and one which its inhabitants thought unique. But after a while Mike realised 'every tidal creek attracted approximately the same type of character'. The next creek up the Crouch is Fenn Creek. Here lived an architect who had built his own wooden home with a complete glass front that overlooked the water. He could dive into the creek at High Water from his living-room window. Fenn's sea veteran was a retired square rig captain who on spring tides loaded his firewood onto the kitchen table to keep it dry as his floor would be under water.

Vagrant was what was called a 'rise-on'. She had started life as an open beach boat at Leigh-on-Sea. Then she'd had her topsides built up by 2 feet before being decked over. She had once been a cutter, but then 'converted' to a sloop. Mike's maiden voyage in her was with a refugee from the Hungarian Revolution called Gabor and an old mucker from his army days in North Africa. Their sole 'how to' guide on board was the 25p Pelican paperback *Sailing* by Peter Heaton. It had a foreword by Vice-Admiral Sir Geoffrey Blake, KCB, DSO Vice Commodore of the Royal Navy Sailing

Mike, Kath and Hilary boarding *Vagrant*

Kath at the helm of *Vagrant* with Hilary in cot

Association, who wrote: '...occasionally there is a diffidence in embarking on some-thing you know little about'. But Mike did not read forewords. In any case there was nothing in the book about rise-ons and the boat ran wonderfully well in a fresh breeze down to Shore Ends at the mouth of the Crouch. Here they tried to turn round and come back up river, but the removal of *Vagrant*'s bowsprit and jib had made her unwieldy and with their inexperience they couldn't get her about. Peter Heaton's warning that 'you will never do any good with a badly balanced hull. Further, it might prove dangerous,' was academic now as *Sailing* was so much papier-mâché in the swilling bilges. So they ran on as the wind increased and Gabor, who had taken greater care of his English–Hungarian dictionary than Mike had of *Sailing*, desperately flicked through its pages before yelling: 'Puddle, puddle' and pointed down below. The boat's centre-board case was leaking badly through the plate bolt, Mike did his best to 'caulk' the worn hole with a spare cheese sandwich: a tough decision for a man with Mike's appetite, but he considered it was that or enjoy a last supper. They baled furiously and continued through the Rays'n Channel towards the nearest downwind terra firma at West Mersea where they piled up with great relief.

But Mike was hooked. 'As a maiden voyage it was memorable and the start of a way of life.' For many years he proudly kept a news cutting from a local paper which reported how racing had been cancelled locally because of strong winds that day. A testament of adventure even greater than bog-trotting.

After that first sail he took out a young man who kept a centre-boarder in the creek – Gordon Hamilton – to show him the ropes. 'After a while, Mike asked me if I was hungry. Then he pulled a stale crust of bread out of his dirty old anorak, broke it in two and gave me half. I thought it was a bit odd,' Gordon recalled. Gordon advised Mike to re-rig *Vagrant* as a cutter, which he did. All these incidents would re-emerge many years later as cartoons inhabited by Mike's alter egos. But at the time yachting magazines felt their readership must not be mocked. 'Sailing was a serious business. Ensigns were hoisted at daybreak and were struck at sunset. In proper yachting circles, standards were upheld. The inhabitants of Clements Green Creek wallowing in primeval mud did not have them,' said Mike, who could have 'papered a room' with rejection slips from the yachting press.

The first anchorage discovered by Mike, Kath and baby Hilary was Pyefleet Creek behind East Mersea. They adored its solitude, its steep-to pebble beach where Hilary's feet could be dipped in the tide, and its lonely marshes. The first time they anchored there they shared the shelter with seven auxiliary sailing barges: their topmasts gone, replaced with 'iron topsails' (engines) and unwittingly watched the end of trading sail. Essex had already been described as 'The Last Stronghold of Sail' by Hervey Benham and it had hung on so long thanks to the efficient spritsail rig which enabled two men to sail 200 tons of freight anywhere from Great Yarmouth to the Solent and much farther afield in the Thames sailing barges' heyday.

Pyefleet is the same today as it was all those years ago and Mike can be found anchored there in winter and summer still.

His learning curve continued when *Vagrant* ran aground on the ebb one evening as he cut off a bend of the River Colne known as Hyde Park Corner. Cursing his luck he was later chastened to learn that another yacht – which had remained afloat that same night – had been run down by a Colchester-bound coaster and her two crew drowned. Her 'tinny riding light' had either not been spotted or more likely blown out. Mike replaced his own with the more powerful Tilley lamp. He still uses one to this day.

While sailing solo on the Blackwater one day, Mike ran aground on Thirslet Spit. It was nearly low water so he pulled on his sea-boots and, using the dinghy as a walking frame, started sliding across the ooze to the shoreline in order to telephone Kath and let her know when he'd be home. He came across a wildfowler in a gun punt who asked him where he was going. Mike told him. 'Give me her number. I'll

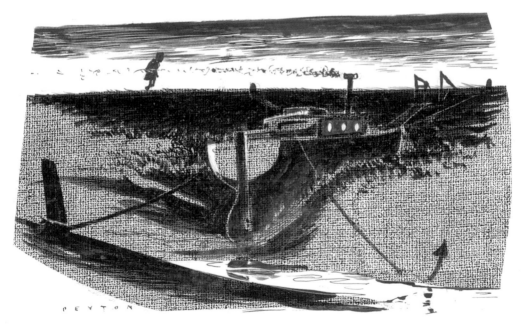

PEYTON

do it. You get back to your boat.' It was good advice for the flood had started and the mud was getting softer. The 'duck shooter', as Mike described him, did call Kath to put her mind at rest and from that day on the arrangement was that Kath would never expect a call while Mike was away.

Nevertheless it did not completely relieve her of worry. 'I remember standing on top of the hill looking away down the river for the sign of a sail when Mike was overdue (as on many occasions) from several days at sea.' That hill has now disappeared: it was bulldozed away to make the new town of South Woodham Ferrers which stands there today.

Vagrant drew one foot six inches with her plate up. They liked this last dimension, having learnt at least the one vital fact of life concerning local yachting: that a beginner spent more time going aground than in actual sailing. She had a large cockpit, two berths in the saloon, and a small galley. There was an engine, which did not work. Neither Mike or Kath are mechanically minded and decided straight away not to bother with it. By now they had discovered a mentor more suited to the peculiarities of East Coast sailing than Peter Heaton, who was really a Solent man. Maurice Griffiths's book *Ten Small Yachts* was also a hardback and therefore likely to disintegrate more slowly than Heaton's paperback in *Vagrant*'s leaking bilges. They were reassured to learn that the first three of the ten yachts weren't even fitted with an engine. Maurice was writing about yachting in the early 1930s when it was a comparative rarity for a sailing boat to have an engine, and other sailing people, and harbour officials acted accordingly. As unwitting 'purists' they were to learn later that the top end of a drying creek was not the ideal mooring place for a boat without any auxiliary power. Yet Hilary watched from her pram on the sea wall at Clements Green Creek while her parents laid a mooring for *Vagrant*. It involved digging a large hole in liquid mud, a fascinating East Coast occupation. When her parents climbed back up the sea wall to feed their baby daughter she burst into tears at the sight of two figures dripping in black ooze. Kath knew just how she felt.

Vagrant was neither nippy nor fast, rolled horribly in a sea, and they spent many hours tacking arduously up or down our narrow home water, getting to know every knob and wrinkle of its pitted banks. Many times they had to anchor when the water ran out on them, and struggle ashore through the mud with the carrycot slung between them. Kath looks back on this with horror, although at the time it was all part of sailing.

'To buy a five-tonner and be your own skipper without any initial crewing on somebody else's boat, with only a 'How-to-do-it' book at the ready on the cockpit seat as you skate from one crisis to another, is not the best way to learn. I might add that it is probably the quickest, and the most exciting and, with a six-month-old baby laughing at you, the most nerve-wracking. The very first time we went out it was blowing hard, which we thought very suitable. Only one other sail was to be seen on the river. "What a funny boat," I commented as we creamed down the creek. Now we know that it was a ketch, travelling fast under staysail and mizzen alone. We had no reefs in at all, and when we got out of the shelter of the creek, *Vagrant* took charge completely. She had what we later learnt was 'weather helm,' and Mike could not hold her. Like a bolting horse, she went up the sea wall and broke her rudder. Damage or no, I was merely glad that she had stopped.'

Kath, Mike and Hilary row to *Vagrant*

Hilary in her bunk

'By Jove, Maurice, I fairly got the wind up out there but it's jolly to be in here now,' a crew confides in *Ten Small Yachts*. Kath's language to Mike after each hard-learned lesson came with more emphasis. But the cartoon bank was building nicely. It was while he owned *Vagrant* that Mike's venture into sartorial elegance came to an end. One windy day returning home from his London duty he went straight down to the creekside to check on his boat. To his horror a big tide had stretched the rising chain of his dinghy to its limit and waves were starting to slop over the gunnels. Mike waded straight in to rescue his tender and ruined his tweed suit.

Kath remembers the humiliation of making fools of themselves in front of people who already knew how to sail, of not knowing what to do, not knowing which way to push the tiller. 'Not even to know the infuriating jargon – I hated it at times, and at times I was frightened, a real sick fear that I had never experienced before. I knew nothing, and I also knew that Mike knew little more, and we had the child with us.'

The following summer there was another one too. Another girl. Mike, visualising useful crew, groaned when he heard the news. The four of them spent a fortnight in high summer that year pottering between Maldon, Tollesbury, Mersea and Brightlingsea. *Vagrant* was festooned with nappies, and taking the ground wherever possible so that the new parents could relax a little from the vigilance of making sure the children did not fall overboard.

'We want something a bit bigger,' Mike said. 'Every time I put Veronica over my shoulder to pat her back I bang her head on the deck beams.' Hilary's very first sentence was, 'Mind my head,' uttered when her father lifted her into the bunk-bed he had made for her under the deckhead over Kath's berth. It had all of 18 inches headroom. But really Mike wanted a bigger boat to go farther afield.

Before he sold her, two colleagues from *The New Scientist* joined Mike aboard *Vagrant* during several bitterly cold February weekends to test out a new survival suit for an article. Anchored in the Crouch, drinking tea, they ran out of matches so one of the journalists, dressed in a suit, swam across to a nearby angling boat and asked its occupant for a light. The angler, though astonished, handed him a box of matches which he zipped into his suit before swimming back.

The following spring Mike sold *Vagrant* to an importer of bananas who wanted her based at Tewkesbury. Mike agreed to help *Vagrant's* new skipper sail her as far as London and from there he would be left to make the rest of the passage through the Grand Union Canal. Because he was selling the boat Mike had had the engine overhauled and it was now quite reliable.

On the night the new owner arrived to take delivery, there were floods all over the South East, and it was impossible even to leave the house, as the water was right up to the back door. The electric light went out, and they all sat eating bananas by candlelight.

Vagrant's passage up the Thames was through a river full of floating flotsam after the floods, and the propeller kept getting fouled. When they reached St Katharine's Dock late on Sunday night, they discovered it had been closed for two years, and the police told them they would have to proceed up to Chelsea and leave the boat there. This meant taking the mast out. *Vagrant's* new owner was by then getting frantic to return to Birmingham for the early morning trade in bananas, so he left, and Mike completed the journey up to Chelsea, hitching a tow from a tug. Since leaving her home county, '*Vagrant* has travelled quite extensively having been based on the Severn, at Poole and the last we heard of her, in North Wales'.

· 9 ·

Hiscock in the Swatchways

The East Coast had started to work its magic on the Peytons and they coveted a boat with character. Thames barges – by now virtually obsolete – were being laid up by the score: hulked in creeks, broken up or converted into floating homes. They could be bought then for a few hundred pounds. But Mike, who has never been keen on maintenance, did not relish an LOA of 80 feet. Smacks had already ended their working days and many were already hulked and covered in seaweed as they filled with each tide. Those which were left were considered a good alternative to having a yacht built and therefore beyond Mike's price range.

At this time the Peytons had stopped using their local pub, The Railway, in South Woodham Ferrers, because they had discovered The Ferry Boat Inn at North Fambridge. The old weatherboard pub with its duck pond stood alone behind the sea wall with only boats propped up on stilts for company and just a few minutes' walk from the River Crouch. The talk beneath its low, beamed ceilings was dominated by sailing. The Ferry Boat became their local and still is today.

It was in the tap room one evening Mike learned from a yachtsman who had just returned from Holland that, with the damming of the Zuider Zee some 20 years before, the former saltwater bay had gradually become a fresh water lake killing the fishing industry. Many former fishing ports were becoming inland towns and trawlers were being made redundant. Like the obsolete Thames barges, there were many for sale on the cheap, but unlike the Thames barges they were half the size. Without a second thought Mike packed a chart and a hand-bearing compass in his kitbag and with a potential crew took the ferry to Holland. The potential crew had a Dutch friend who spoke good English and owned a car so the trio swiftly looked at dozens of botters which all had tarred hulls except for one which was varnished, EB 49 in the one-time Hanseatic port of Elburg, now becoming a landlocked tourist attraction with just a canal linking it to the dead IJsselmeer. Mike deduced that the 40 ft EB 49 must be in good condition: anyone proud enough to varnish his craft in a world where tar was the norm would be someone who looked after his vessel. He had not registered at the time the two 'hulking sons' the botter owner had to help him keep her up to scratch. However Mike's offer was turned down and he returned to Essex.

'Michael always acts on things most people would just sit at home and think about,' said Kath, who had doubts about buying such an exotic craft when he showed her photographs he had taken.

'To me she looked medieval, like something out of a Van der Neer painting, and in essence, of course, she was. The essential Dutch shape had remained much the same for centuries,' she said.

She had enormous bluff bows and beam, a comparatively fine stern, and shallow draught. She had an unstayed mast, which came up out of the keel 'like a growing tree'. Aft of the mast she was just one big fish well; the water came through plates in her bottom, so that the fish were kept alive until ready to market. Before the mast she was decked over, which made a cabin 12 ft x 14 ft. Her sails were good: gaff mainsail, staysail and jib. The bowsprit ran inboard if necessary.

It was October by the time the price, £400, had been agreed and Peter Small, one of *The New Scientist* journalists who had worked with Mike on the survival suit special, joined his old skipper to bring the botter home. She was powered by a Kromhaut diesel engine, dated 1913, which they both looked at with misgivings. Once clear of the North Sea Canal it coughed and died. Peter was no more of an engine man than Mike and after beating vainly into a head wind for a day and getting nowhere, they returned to IJmuiden and came home on the steamer.

When Mike returned for the botter it was with two other yachtsmen. The first was Gordon Hamilton, who had sailed with Mike in *Vagrant*, and who moored his 18 ft double-ended cutter, *Snipe* – once owned by the legendary yachtsman, author and journalist F B Cooke – in a Clements Green Creek mud berth in winter, and on a swinging mooring at Fambridge in summer. Gordon had sailed his little boat solo to Ostend several times. The third member of the crew was a friend of Gordon's, John Barstow, an ex-Royal Navy lieutenant who turned up in a white riding mac and bobble hat. He was a Winchester and Oxford man, tall and thin with a long white face and a languid air, which proved deceptive.

Whatever their fears about bringing an unknown boat across the North Sea in November, they had not counted on being becalmed. Kath waited at home, as one still, misty day succeeded another.

She walked to the top of the hill that overlooked the creek and stood there, looking for a sail down the wide valley as the tide crept in. But the only thing that moved were the sheep bleating on the sea wall. After three days she began to worry, but on the fourth day the telephone rang, 'We're in Faversham.'

'Faversham'? I thought Faversham was in Kent?'

'Yes...well, it's England, anyway.'

The trip across had been uneventful, save for the errors of navigation that had landed them in Kent instead of Essex. Having picked up the Outer Gabbard, they had then had a spanking sail down to what they had intended to be the Sunk, but which turned out to be the Kentish Knock instead. The botter made more leeway than they had supposed, they also discovered that the one wrist watch between them was two hours out, which had affected the allowances made for tides. Suspecting this, they had gone close to the Kentish Knock lightship to ask the time. It was dark, and the botter was travelling fast. Light spilled out of an open door on the lightship as silhouetted figures watched and responded to a yelled request for a time check: 'What ship are you?'

The botter was as yet unnamed and Mike – never good with figures – could not remember the official number.

'I don't know,' he yelled back helplessly and as he did so he could feel the look of bewilderment on the lightship crew's faces as the two silhouettes turned to one another before the door closed. The nameless botter pressed on under billowing

The Ferry Boat Inn, Mike's local, where his sailing pal asked for his beer belly to be 'filled up'

brown canvas, the timeless Trinity House ship remained under the sweep of her light. Ships that pass in the night. It would make a great cartoon.

The following weekend, there was no lack of Clements Green Creekers to help sail the boat back to the Crouch with a southwesterly Force 7 trapped in her cloths. On Sunday, the storm had blown itself out.

Kath stood at her usual post on the hill over the creek to see if her husband was returning. 'I saw her drifting up the creek, her sails goose-winged, her long red bob dropping against the grey sky. I stared at her with all the pride of possession in me: she was the most beautiful boat I had ever set eyes on.'

Later Kath was awed at the boat's scale. Her oak frames were seven inches square, her oak planking two inches thick. When her staysail went to the sail makers for overhauling it took two men to lift it off the deck. Everything on board was a major sweat of hauling, from her anchor and leeboards to her mainsail; her mainsheet block was the size of a man's head. Her high, bluff bows, the characteristic that distinguishes the botter from most of the other types of Dutch boat, made it difficult for the helmsman to see ahead and in the river it meant that a lookout was a necessary member of the crew. And all members of the crew needed muscle.

It was later to become a standing joke that anyone who sailed on board EB 49 earned his Botter Campaign Medal, with oak leaves, if they came again.

They named her *Clementine*, the closest they could get to the sound of her official number which Mike had forgotten mid-North Sea.

When the children went aboard, there was more danger of their drowning in the fish well than over the side.

The trunk of the fish well was like a rectangular box with sides about three feet high and with water inside. It took up most of the space aft of the mast, and would have to be removed if she was to be converted into a yacht. A start was made by replacing the fish well's through-hull limber holes with planking. Though as they did not caulk between the new planking the fish well was as efficient as ever. The cabin was vast compared to *Vagrant*'s. It had a little door, in two parts like a stable-door; towards the bows there was a big step up about two feet high, like a gigantic shelf, and on this communal bunk several people could sleep in comfort. 'Generally you had ample room, but there were times when you all had to turn over together.' But it was the right boat for a coal stove and Mike's first job was to get one installed. Now he had his own smoking chimney among the motley collection of craft in Clements Green Creek.

'It became an accepted moan in the village that when *Clementine*'s engine was playing up, no one else's cars, tractors, motor-mowers or bacon-slicers got a look in as far as the local mechanic was concerned,' said Kath, 'Although we ran it on diesel oil, it could run on coconut oil as well, and it was started with touch-papers and a match, which we used to call "putting the fireworks in"'. When it was running, it used to throw up black smoke rings from its exhaust, which stood up just in front of where the helmsman stood, at eye-level.

But *Clementine* was first and foremost a sailing boat. The Force 7 of her homecoming weekend was, her crew agreed, exactly her cup of tea. Her great bows just sat on the confusion of the estuary sea and she kept on going, barge-fashion, scarcely heeling. With a fair wind she would bowl along, pushing up a flurry of foam under her blunt stem, her long bob streaming above the curved gaff. She attracted a good deal of attention, and by the time summer came her crew were used to sailing along under the gaze of several pairs of binoculars, and to being boarded by complete strangers, full of enthusiasm. *Clementine* always seemed to be full of people, and was often sailing with small boats towing astern, which belonged to people who wanted to have a go.

After barely three years the Peytons still had a great deal to learn about sailing, and their mistakes were never made in anonymous oblivion. One weekend a neighbour asked the tyros if they could go down to the mouth of the river where he had a steel lifeboat on an anchor and tow it home up the creek for him. Tom Bolton worked in London docks and was always bringing home 'bargains'.

The lifeboat was an open steel boat, 40 ft long, which Tom had brought round from Tilbury Dock the previous weekend. The boat had no engine or sails. But after a tow from a barge as far as Southend, Tom set a sheet of tarpaulin, and using a long sweep for steering and sustaining himself with tea from a Thermos flask he had drifted on the tide until, in the darkness, had gone ashore on Foulness.

Wrapped in the tarpaulin he spent a bitter night in the bottom of the boat, before getting a second tow from a fishing boat to the mouth of the Crouch.

Clementine's engine was not working again but Mike's doubts about acting as a tug were allayed by the fair wind and tide they now had. Plus he had a press gang of willing hands from Clements Green Creek and once through Burnham there would be nothing to worry about.

Over a thousand yachts were moored in the river off the red brick Georgian houses of Burnham waterfront, the Cowes of the East Coast. Even the fairway on the south side of the river was very congested in those days. The yachts moored

Clementine ashore in Essex for caulking

there were expensive, with gleaming topsides, in no way the kind to be nudged by a passing botter.

The 40 ft Dutch botter towing a 40 ft steel lifeboat set off with a strong reaching wind ideal for the job at hand. It was late afternoon, with a bright sun glossing the river with Sunday goodwill; everyone was coming home on the tide with shining red faces, well content, and on the motor yachts tea was being served out of the wind. Most of the big yachts were home, and were being tidied up: 'Hand the burgee, Tarquin'. But the wind was dropping lighter. Mike began to look slightly anxious as he worked out his way ahead, to keep her going meant freeing off and picking a line through the moorings, the skylarking stopped and everyone went quiet as they drifted into a major cartoon.

In a matter of minutes the wind died completely. From a cracking reach that had taken the motley convoy roaring three-quarters of the way past the moorings, they were now merely carrying their way.

The great board of the mainsail caved in. They looked round anxiously as the steel tender came up and nudged them like a playful puppy. Straight ahead of them were two of the glossiest yachts in Burnham, and alongside, cutting them off from the fairway, were two more. Three of these yachts had people on board, and they were watching, not saying anything, very calm and expressionless. Twenty-three tons of oak botter and 40 feet of steel lifeboat moved inexorably towards them, and one of the men got out a little canvas fender three inches in diameter and hung it over his quarter: all the details seared into Mike's brain. He would exorcise them years later on the drawing board.

'Anchor,' he said.

Kath went below, in a sweat of horror, and heard the urgent rush of feet over her head and the clanks and thumps as the enormous grapnel anchor went out on its warp. Nobody was saying anything. Once the anchor had gone, there was silence. *Clementine* drifted on, the feet clumped back aft. The anchor took up. Mike said, 'Pull the lifeboat up alongside'.

Very calmly, as if it was a rubber dinghy, Tom pulled his lifeboat up on her painter and walked forward. Kath stood at the stable door watching and, as *Clementine* turned into the tide, saw Tom clear his lifeboat from the yacht with the fender with two inches to spare. The owners of the yacht were still standing there, stoney-eyed, very polite, not saying anything. 'I thought Tom was going to raise his hat.'

The anchor held, in spite of its short scope. *Clementine* drifted back and lay exactly in the middle of the square formed by the four big yachts. Mike was able to lay out another fathom or two of warp, Tom made the lifeboat fast alongside, the rest of the crew dropped the sails and then all hands went below. 'Put the kettle on,' said Mike, he was grinning. *Clementine* was uninsured.

'It was always my habit to go below when crisis loomed up, unless I was actually given a job. Although aware that this was pure cowardice, and feeling properly ashamed, I could not help myself. I have since found out that this reaction to crisis is nothing unique', said Kath. Another Clements Green Creeker skippered a 38 foot cutter and he was inclined to do the same thing, unless closely watched. John Barstow was once crewing for him when, approaching Ramsgate, in a strong southwesterly, he was horrified to see his skipper disappear down the companion-way when the yacht was through the harbour entrance. She had everything set and was charging straight for the stone wall of the harbour. John, though little experienced, never panicked, and cast off every sheet in sight, and let all the halyards fly, so that sails and spars fell in all directions and the yacht slowed up from trawling all her gear over the side. 'It may not have been seamanlike,' John later explained to a fascinated Mike, 'but it stopped her'.

Clementine lay anchored among the now deserted yachts, as though by design. Through the calm dusk, Kath sat watching the tide sliding past. The clock tower in Burnham High Street noted each hour with its tinny chime. Lights started coming on along the quay.

This was not the first time Kath had been petrified by *Clementine*'s potential to do damage; Mike, on the other hand, was exhilarated by the problems she set. When the wind came up again, with the next flood he enjoyed working out the moves to winkle her out of her delicate situation. The obvious consequences of making a mistake added to, rather than detracted from, the situation. It had once been the same on mountains.

'I shared his enthusiasm then, but on boats I did not feel the same. On boats I went below and put a cushion over my head. Lovely as *Clementine* was, she was too big, I thought,' said Kath.

Mike agreed but not because of the sailing, but because of the maintenance he faced. The following summer was a very hot one, and *Clementine*, in common with many of the older boats on the river, opened up her seams and started to leak. They had to beach her and Mike spent hours banging in oakum while Kath watched the children playing over the saltings, in and out of the water. The seams that leaked were the ones just above the waterline.

'Each one is 40 feet long,' said Mike gloomily, 'That's 80 feet, both sides, and the ones above...120, 160 feet'.

He hammered away morosely. Every day was hotter than the one before, as he hammered on.

'She needs rubbing down and revarnishing,' Kath pointed out.

'Huh.'

During a cruise to Kent the engine would not work, the mainsail developed a tear and in a sudden squall *Clementine* heeled over enough to make water through a seam above the ones Mike had recaulked. They beached her again and Kath sewed while Mike hammered. They pottered about the Swale in the heat and the quiet. They lay in the ooze of Oare Creek as sheep bleated in a heat-haze in the fields behind the sea wall. More seams opened up in the glaring sun.

'Behind us in the Thames the big shipping thumped over the still water, with mirage-like reflections. An oil tanker was making for the Swale. We were in the creek with the quants out, poling, very medieval, but enjoying the soft thrust in the mud, the barefoot pad back along the hot deck and the gentle progress, snail-like, to Faversham. We could smell the diesel stench of the tanker, thudding up the Swale, and I was glad we were out of the way, in the off-shoot of the creek.'

They rested on their quant poles in the heat, the bleat of hot sheep ahead of them and the thump of the tanker astern.

'It's coming up here,' Kath said, as a joke.

But then the thump drowned out the bleats.

'Start punting,' Mike said, as the big steel bows bore down on them, pushing over a glassy bow wave. They were amazed that the little, winding, sheep-fringed Faversham Creek was a highway for oil tankers. The tanker swept past and *Clementine* went aground on its wash, the children chortling at the sudden excitement. At a fork of the creek a little farther on, the tanker turned round, 'delicate as a cat' in the

Wanderer III aground on Foulness Sand

confined space, and continued her journey through the Kentish fields in reverse. The crew of the botter poled on more cautiously, with many backward glances.

Late that season Mike had a weekend away with John Barstow and they pottered about the Crouch and Roach. Sailing up the latter they spotted a smart white sloop anchored in Yokesfleet Creek. John got the binoculars trained on this stranger to their world. She had wide decks and a transom stern...and then John, catching his breath, read her name: *Wanderer III*. 'My God it's Hiscock,' he said. Indeed it was the legendary Solent-based cruising man with his wife Susan on an East Coast visit. Of his first visit to the East Coast, in his gaff cutter *Wanderer III*, Hiscock wrote: 'we were well familiar with such fascinating names as the Kentish Knock, Barrow Deep, and Shivering Sand, Rays'n Channel, Paglesham and Mersea Quarters but they were names only from our Maurice Griffiths and our Francis B Cooke. We had never done any cruising in those parts and our education had been sadly neglected.' Their East Coast education came thick and fast as soon as they rounded the North Foreland for they narrowly missed hitting the East Last Sand en route to Harty Ferry, from there to Burnham they did hit the Columbine and the same day ran hard aground on Foulness Sand while tacking up the Crouch on a falling tide. 'The angry little seas, blown with churned up sand, slapped *Wanderer*'s weather quarter and hissed along her lee deck and degree by degree as the tide fell she listed further and further.' Hiscock sat gloomily below listening to the cups clinking as they slid and hit one another and the books in his library slapping together as they fell over, wondering how much further she would go over. 'With night coming on and the glass falling the outlook was gloomy, we stepped out on to the hard wrinkled sand and there the tide had left her, our poor boat lay at a forlorn angle on a huge expanse of sand.'

But Mike and John had no idea how wary Hiscock was of the East Coast as they sailed towards *Wanderer III*, this time happily afloat in a snug anchorage. Instead John was full of admiration, and a sense of occasion, having read the Hiscock books and articles. As they got nearer they could see Hiscock standing in the cockpit. John could not resist hailing him with friendly congratulations about his writing. 'He had albino colouring,' Mike recalled, 'white hair and very pale skin'. So the fact he went bright scarlet before disappearing below was even more marked. John was disappointed but could not know that his cruising guru was still chastened by his East Coast learning curve.

By the end of the season Mike had had enough of caulking, sandpapering and varnishing, and this was before they'd even started on converting her.

'We'll get something smaller, that just the two of us can handle,' he said.

Prospective buyers of a botter were as 'characterful' as the boats themselves.

'The odd admiral was as likely to turn up among the artists as the wistful carpenter with a £10 downpayment. Our garden on a Sunday was dotted with ancient motorbikes, vintage Rolls, yellow bull-nosed Morrises and broken-down vans,' Kath recalls.

Most were put off by the workload, too. But one Sunday two separate parties appeared, one on foot and one by Rolls Royce, and both wanted to buy her. 'The Rolls Royce got his deposit in first, but when the sale was just about to be completed, and everyone else turned away, he got cold feet and withdrew, leaving us back where we had started from. A little later we heard he'd bought a Silhouette,' said Kath.

The other party had been so angry at losing *Clementine*, he had shouted down the telephone at her owners. 'Mike's northern pigheadedness asserted itself and he refused to get in touch with him again, but fortunately he found out about the circumstances from another source and a week later the deal was completed.' Humphrey, who signed the cheque, was a copywriter. He arranged to come down on a Thursday evening to take possession.

'Let's go down and make her look nice,' Kath said on Wednesday.

They walked down to the creek across the fields, *Clementine*'s long red bob, frayed now and faded, fluttered against the sky.

She lay comfortably in a niche in the saltings, surrounded at low tide by

Clementine looked 'medieval' according to Kath

springy wastes of sea lavender. On that Wednesday the tide was high. They stood on the sea wall and looked at *Clementine*, their moment of sentiment turning abruptly to horror. Through a hole in her side a great spout of water was steadily pouring. With a bucket each they baled steadily until the tide went down and the boat was dry, then Mike started his oakum hammering again. A big lump had worked out below the waterline.

'Not a word to Humphrey,' Kath said nervously.

'No. But he knows she wants recaulking,' Mike said, 'He knows what he's in for.'

When Humphrey arrived the next evening, he settled himself in the armchair and said, 'A strange thing happened to me last night'.

'Oh?' they looked non-committal.

'I went to a party,' Humphrey said, 'In Chelsea. There was a man there who makes a living by foretelling the future, clairvoyance or whatever it is. So just for a lark I told him I'd bought a boat. I asked him if it was any good.'

'What did he say?' Kath asked.

'I didn't tell him what sort of boat it was, I just said a boat. But he said, "Yes, I can see it. It's very big at the front and brown all over. A mast, and on the left side, opposite the mast, there's a hole and the water is coming in." Fantastic, wasn't it?' Humphrey said, beaming. 'I mean, big at the front and brown all over is *Clementine* all right.'

Mike and Kath stared at him. It was even more fantastic than he thought. Candidly they told him what had happened and it was his turn to stare. 'We all sat and looked at each other, awed,' Kath recalled, 'Our first personal experience of psychic power, we found it very impressive.'

Mike's reaction was more practical: 'He'd make a fortune if he set up as a surveyor'.

• 10 •

Going Foreign

Without a boat, Mike was like Dracula at the onset of dawn. He made frantic weekend trips in the cars of Clements Green Creekers to Woodbridge, Dover and the Hamble. His journeys taught him that a decent boat was really beyond his means, but this just galvanised him into further denial. Saving 'like misers', living on mutton stew and with just the clothes they stood up in, Mike told his wife in their bare home with her bare wardrobe: 'First things first'. All the children's clothes were re-cut by Kath from adult cast offs. When a neighbour replaced her washing machine, the original – 20 years old – was installed at Long Acre. Their carpet and three piece suite was a second-hand job lot from the market. 'I often thought I was very lucky that we had bought the house before the first boat,' Kath recalled drily.

Sugar Creek was an 11-ton Norwegian-built, Colin Archer designed gaff cutter, built in 1930, 30 ft x 10 ft 6 ins x 4 ft 9 ins. Double-ended, she was heavily constructed of pitch pine on oak. The boat had originally belonged to an American who named her after the place where a group of Mormons, driven out of Illinois in 1846 by anti-religious bigots, made their first camp in safety on the west side of the Mississippi, before continuing their trek to Salt Lake City where they flourish today. The American was to have sailed her home across the Atlantic, but never did.

'She'll go anywhere,' said Mike, who had found her at Ramsgate.

'Has she got an engine?' asked his wife, the memory of *Clementine*'s tow still fresh in her mind.

She had a 6hp Sleipner, a Swedish-built contraption which ran, or not as the case was, on a mixture of petrol and paraffin. She was £300 more than their very top limit. But she was the right boat.

'It'll be funny having a boat you can't go aground in. Comfortably, I mean,' said Kath. Both *Vagrant* and *Clementine* had always given them a warning of shoaling waters with centre-board and leeboard respectively, and often enough, to make sure of a quiet night, they had pushed their bows on the mud somewhere.

'And what about keeping her in the creek? She'll lie over.'

'We'll keep her at Fambridge,' Mike said. Fambridge had deep-water moorings out in the River Crouch proper. Here sailed different types of yachtsman: professionals who came down from the city. They included teachers, solicitors, and a Dr Ely who 'rather ruled the roost'. He wore white gloves when sailing and because of this the young Gordon Hamilton thought he looked like Mickey Mouse and expressed his observations to Mr Meiklejohn, the proprietor of the moorings who put him in his place by telling him that Dr Ely was a top surgeon whose fingertips were worth protecting. Another character owned a yawl which, down below, was finished with gloss varnish on the starboard side which was to the skipper's liking and matt on the port side which the co-owner preferred.

Beric at Fambridge Yacht Club HQ, designed for use as a field hospital during the Boer War

At Fambridge, Kath became acquainted with *Sugar Creek*'s four inch frames and one and a quarter inch planking. She had a galley that together with a head took up the whole of her large forepeak, which would become the children's quarters. There were two bunks in the saloon, which had standing headroom, then a bulkhead separated off the after part which had two quarter berths, and the engine installed out of the way under the bridgedeck. There was a steep companionway leading up to a deep, small cockpit.

In the five years they owned *Sugar Creek*, they added improvements as they could afford them. The first season the garboards were splined, the galley moved aft, taking the place of the port-side quarter-berth. The forepeak was fitted with two bunks built with high sides. She could then sleep five in comfort, and seven at a pinch, using the cabin sole. There were roomy lockers in the saloon behind the bunks, with varnished doors; they painted the deckhead, the forepeak and the after part white to give more light. Mike replaced the companionway with a single wooden step over the hefty flywheel, adding more space to the saloon. He also installed the obligatory coal-stove. Her bilge was ballasted with concrete blocks fitted with rings so they could be lifted out. Some of it Mike replaced with lead, as he could afford it. The galley was simple, two Primuses in gimbals, and a washbowl flush with the work surface. Fresh water was carried in plastic jerry cans. Mike, in true Thoreau-style, discarded the flushing lavatory as an unnecessary complication with problematic sea-cocks and replaced it with a bucket.

Kath loved the teak-laid deck, but it leaked and Mike wanted to paint it with an old recipe – which included molasses – he'd found in a barging book. But after they were recaulked Kath kept her bare planks.

Sugar Creek had no guard rail, just a toerail amidships. They had the bulwarks raised, first of all to a point several feet short of her stem, but later right round and

In dry dock, *Sugar Creek* gets some caulking from Peter Pointer

a guard rail fitted which Kath draped with rope pig-netting to stop the girls going over the side. A pulpit was a 'vast comfort', in fact in those days it was a rare appendage. When Mike fitted one to a later boat he had it stood on deck ready to mark up the bolt-holes when a curious pal, passing in a dinghy, grabbed it and dropped it over the side. They had to grapple for it. *Sugar Creek* also had a metal boom gallows behind the cockpit, with strong bolts fastening it into the deck, so that they could lean on it, and make fast to it with confidence. Coamings from the after corners of the cabin top were enlarged; they went right round the cockpit, leaving a shelf to sit on, and making the bridgedeck into a handy sitting place.

Her mast was tall enough to have rigged her bermudian, instead Mike filled the space with a topsail which made a big difference to her performance. She carried a staysail and a jib, and at times a flying jib. They painted her blue-grey, and her bulkwarks black; her big rubbing strake and capping-rail were varnished.

At Long Acre there was a beer glass filled with cash. When it dropped below half full Mike would be obliged to start drawing cartoons again and this usually entailed lying on the sofa with a newspaper over his head as Gordon Hamilton once observed when he called round. 'Don't interrupt Mike,' Kath said, 'he's working.' Mike also dreamed up cartoon ideas in the bath, although that came later when he could afford the hot water.

Even in June the wind, when it comes from the north-east, is cold and it's an 11 mile dead plug to get out of the River Crouch from Burnham and into the North Sea. These were the conditions that year for their first cruise. *Sugar Creek* drew four feet nine inches and therefore the sand-muzzled Rays'n Channel was denied them until an hour or so each side of High Water. Instead they had to beat on to the Spitway, the alternative buoyed channel through the Buxey and Gunfleet sands.

It was dusk by the time they cleared the Outer Crouch, and the wind, dead on the nose, was steadily growing stronger. The sky was full of stars, and the light of the South Buxey, marking the channel between the Foulness and Buxey Sands, winked steadily, two every ten. The South Buxey, 3 miles out from the Outer Crouch, was the only lit buoy off the mouth of the river. *Sugar*, as they called her, made wide, dogged tacks, the dark sail swinging over against the stars.

'I had never sailed at night before. The Tilley lamp hissed below, filling the saloon with its comforting light, brushing the face of the sleeping child in the quarter-berth. The very glimpse of that utterly dependent, curled up, sleeping child, one pudgy hand curled under her cheek, gave me a heavy sense of responsibility. The sea swirled past in the darkness, white tops breaking, and the child slept in the shell of her bunk; sitting on the bridgedeck I could see one and then the other, and the excitement and the tenderness were all mixed up,' said Kath.

The buoy flashed on the port bow. In the thin starlight the sands of Foulness Island gleamed serenely above a hissing line of breaking water.

'We're not getting anywhere very fast,' Mike said. 'I think the tide's turned.'

'Already?'

'We'll go back. And we'll go a lot faster,' Mike freed off the sheets, and the bowsprit slipped round. *Sugar* turned her back on the flashing buoy, and the plunging, crashing motion of a hard beat turned into the smooth ride of a dead run. With wind and tide running in together, the sea rolled towards the shore, and *Sugar* rode up as the waves passed under her.

'The surge beneath her wooden hull had a frightening power; sometimes the tops would break and go hissing forward along the sides of the hull; then she would drop crazily as the next trough opened out, smooth and inviting with shining glassy slopes. I held on to the coamings, not knowing whether to be frightened or not. It was certainly exhilarating, skating through this hissing dark with the mast rolling and the boom-end skimming perilously close to the water; it was dangerous too, which we sensed, but did nothing to rectify, comforted by the feeling that we were running for home and would shortly be in the river. This of course is when accidents usually happen to yachts, and we learned fairly soon that running in a strong wind is a far more carefree business under headsails alone, but that night we ran in under full sail, foolish but magnificently excited, storming through the darkness.'

The following morning they set off again. It was calm, hot and slightly hazy, and

"DID YOU CONNECT UP THAT TOILET FRED?"

somewhere in the vicinity of the Ridge buoy the wind died completely. They sat in the hot sun, feeding seagulls, washing clothes, making cups of tea.

By late afternoon the wind picked up and at last they were on their way. The girls were put to bed and *Sugar* lay up the urban coastline of Clacton and Frinton and Walton where the bathing huts were fading into the dusk and the first flash of the Medusa light pierced the sea. They had the tide with them, and round the Naze the wind freshened, it was dark, but the breeze was on their beam, and *Sugar* seemed to be galloping along, at full stretch but easy, with none of the queasy danger of the night's roller-coastering.

But already the wind was dropping lighter. Mike got the chart out to find somewhere to anchor.

'A wall of lights was snaking down the channel; I watched a red navigation light join a green, "One's coming straight towards us," I said, hating the situation, feeling a familiar, bitter, cold fear settling in my stomach. This is sailing, I was thinking: one minute you are galloping along without a care in the world, thinking how marvellous it is; then, within minutes, it can all be changed, all worry and crisis and downright fear. My legs were trembling,' said Kath.

'Shall I go about?'

'No. You watch, she'll carry on round and pass in front of us. Can't you see the channel buoy? We're not in the channel,' said Mike.

The red and green bore inexorably down and Kath was too mesmerised to look for channel buoys. The great thump of the ferry's engines, people leaning over the rail, a door opening and a steward with a trayful of drinks...she was sliding round.

'I realised that I was looking at the side of her, very close, but going past, and nobody was worried but me. It was true we were the right side of the channel buoy.'

They spent the night at anchor in the Rolling Grounds and by dawn Kath, feeling sick and huddled in the cockpit, knew they were accurately named.

By the time they were under way, a thin sun was shining, and the wooded banks of the Stour and the green fields of Constable country slipped down to the wide river and at Wrabness the water was clear.

'Look, a beach,' Kath said to the children, who dropped their toys: bits of driftwood, shells, corks, and strands of seaweed with which they re-created a mini South Woodham Ferrers on the cabin sole: farms and shops and people. They now took up buckets and spades. Wrabness was an enchantment for them, especially when they met a man who had a tame fox which was just as well as Mike was off to London to put in his day's work at *The New Scientist*. Kath lay on the beach watching *Sugar*, wondering what she would do if the boat dragged. 'Let out more chain,' Mike had said. 'But what if I let it all out and she still dragged?'

He got back near midnight, and the wind had freshened from the east. The next morning *Sugar* did drag. 'Damned fisherman's,' Michael said. 'We'll get a CQR.'

Two days later they left Harwich in a dead calm, Mike towing *Sugar* in the dinghy; it was one of those days when the engine did not work.

'It was muggy and glassy, the oars making fussy tracks in the stillness and the drips trailing from the blades as bright as the drops of sweat on Mike's face. Sluggish, but obedient, *Sugar* slipped lethargically on her warp, all her sails hanging. Michael was muttering about catching tides, about the b— wind, and the b— boat, and I was at the tiller, watching the steamers.' All of a sudden, the mainsheet snaked outboard in business-like fashion. Mike grabbed the bobstay, hastily gathered up the towing warp, and scrambled aboard. The sea was bright and beckoning, and now *Sugar* was all out to please, the day transformed by a breath of wind.

'I remembered the same reach, coming in, the dark sea spattered with lights, the bow-wave roaring; now the mysterious *Medusa* was a plain black blob in a glittering, smooth sea: a buoy, no more, no less.' The story of her name is a memorial to Nelson, then sailing a ship of that name, who sent a gig out with seamen armed with leadlines to find an alternative to the deep water channel. It was blowing easterly and he wanted to get out of Harwich. He needed a channel which would give him a slant. He found one and it was named after his ship.

'The story of *Medusa* seemed fanciful now but the night before I would have accepted the *Victory* herself, reaching alongside with her topsails in the stars,' Kath said.

Mike pondered this sailing business: one minute his boat was a stubborn cow on the end of a warp, the next this eager machine, flying for home.

Hilary and Veronica had by now accepted sailing as part of the natural order, not a moment too soon for Mike was eager to go foreign.

'About three months. Not very ambitious. Just short hops down to Falmouth and the Channel Islands, or whatever we feel like,' he said.

'I told him "next year", obeying my natural instinct to procrastinate on such an issue,' Kath recalled, 'I was already realising that Mike was not at heart a family sailing man. He wanted to sail and the children would just have to put up with it, and he had no intention of merely pottering from beach to beach for their benefit. But he was frustrated because the children dictated what he did, whether he liked it or not.'

Late in the summer they took *Sugar* down to Dover. From Ramsgate they slipped past the scoop of Pegwell Bay which was filled with a heat haze, the buoys rolled out on the Goodwins and coasters thumped away. The hypnotic twirling of the log-line spun out astern. The wind dropped lighter and lighter. The line spun more and more slowly, and then stopped for long seconds. The pleasant progress stretched out into tedium. 'We crept under the white cliffs. We ate tea, put the children to bed, sat out in the warm evening and looked at the wall of Dover harbour some half-mile ahead.'

'We're going backwards,' Mike said. 'The tide's turned.'

The anchor went over. 'It must be quite useful, sometimes, to have a reliable engine,' Kath said pointedly.

One of the high spots of cruising for her was the smell of fish and chips wafting over a Kentish harbour: it was one of the great rewards for crossing the estuary. They eventually entered Dover at dawn the next morning, 'One of the few times of day when fish and chips have no appeal,' she said.

'If the weather stays fair, we could go to France,' Mike said, still thinking of going foreign.

France basked, faint and blue, on the horizon. 'Although logic told me that we had just completed a far longer and more difficult trip by crossing from Burnham to Ramsgate, I was nervous about crossing to France,' Kath said.

In Dover, by chance they met the couple from whom they had bought *Vagrant*, Bill and Madge. Madge said Bill had been miserable ever since selling *Vagrant* and they'd come to Dover just to look at the boats.

Mike saw his opportunity: 'How about a trip to Calais then?' Bill's eyes lit up, but Madge was nervous.

'Well, look, we've got the children with us. We're only going if the conditions are ideal.'

The Shipping Forecast next morning gave Thames, Dover, Wight an easterly wind, Force 1 to 2, possibly 3. 'Gusting to 3,' Mike said with great satisfaction. 'Now you can't ask for a gentler passage than that.' The sun was shining; within the walls of the dock the yachts lay motionless, burgees idly lifting with the eternal squawking of the gulls echoing off the slabby grey walls of chalk.

Kath walked up into town to get fresh bread and ham for lunch, on the

"OOPS PARDON, M'SIER"

way back a German youth in shorts with a large rucksack and a rolled black umbrella approached her.

'I look for the yacht haven,' he said. 'It is this way?'

'Come with me. I'll show you.'

Hans had travelled all the way from Schleswig-Holstein to visit the Picasso exhibition in London. 'I felt very humbled, not having been to see it myself. The rolled umbrella was his souvenir of the trip,' said Kath, who was impressed that the young German was looking to hitch a ride back across the Channel. It reminded her of her own early travels.

Sugar Creek left Dover with seven people aboard and butted through a swell towards the French shore that stood out very sharp and blue, beyond a Channel of wild white horses.

'Force 1?' said Kath curiously.

The first wave broke over *Sugar*'s bulwarks and swilled down the deck over Hans's sneakers. He stopped singing 'What shall we do with the drunken sailor' for the children's amusement and looked surprised. *Sugar* was sailing fast, well-heeled, sliding into big green troughs and up through the crests with a crashing of irridescent spray.

'I went below to fetch the ham sandwiches, feeling that if I did not eat them soon I would not eat them at all. I brought out the plateful and put it in the corner of the cockpit, and no sooner had I done so than we shipped a wave that sent them flying, sodden, in all directions. None of us were wearing oilskins. Madge and I were soaked to the skin; the children started to wail, and Hans went on sitting on the cabin-top, ankle-deep in hissing water, and not seeming to care very much.'

'I think we'd better put a reef in,' Mike said to Bill, when all the passengers had retired below. The children were put in their bunks, Madge and Hans took the saloon berths and Kath wedged herself on the floor, feeling glad it was Bill up on deck helping Mike in place of her.

Reefed down, *Sugar* continued her eager ride. It was a day of strong sunshine and glittering seas. The Force 2 had become a Force 5 to 6. Madge was too sick to think about being nervous; twice she was slung out of her bunk across the cabin, and Kath felt that Bill's chances of buying another boat were slipping through his fingers. Hans sat with his head in his hands, reaching for the bucket at intervals. The children were being sick and, in the intervals between attending to them, Kath was too.

'The scene below was like an old engraving of life aboard an emigrant ship. Thank God, we were only emigrating 20 miles,' Kath said.

Such is sailing, the experiences one enjoys least on board make the best stories back on dry land. After they returned home Bill and Madge were regarded in their neighbourhood as something like Cape Horners and, to live up to his reputation, Bill felt bound to buy another boat. A postcard from Hans revealed his nautical hitch-hike as being the high-point of his journey, an adventure much enjoyed in the telling if not in the doing.

The Peytons sat in Calais for three days, during which it rained solidly, and blew a gale. At the end of the week *Sugar Creek* was locked into the inner basin and they all came home on the steamer.

Mike had gone foreign.

• 11 •

Rescue at Sea

May blossom lay like snow across the Crouch valley when *Sugar Creek* and her four crew set off on a planned three-month cruise in easy stages down Channel to Falmouth. At Long Acre the Peytons ate the geese and gave the hens away.

A new mainsail they had ordered was not ready, so the old one was overhauled, and bent on. A new gypsy wheel for the anchor winch had arrived at the last minute and been fitted.

Down below the bunk covers were new and clean, Primuses gleaming. They had spent all the winter weekends working on board. The coal stove had a supply of fuel in the forepeak. It had done good service during the winter, and many cups of tea had been drunk aboard *Sugar Creek* on grey Sunday afternoons. Then the boats at Fambridge wintered in mudberths, and a hard core of owners came down nearly every weekend for these pleasant hammering, tea-drinking sessions, when a cold wind whipped the smoke from the lip of the chimney and the boats pulled at their moorings on the tide. It was not sailing, but it was a part of sailing, the elements blowing under the canvas covers. Now Fambridge has gone modern, and the boats are pulled out to winter in neat rows on a concrete strip. 'One can no longer empty the ashes or the tea dregs over the side, and nobody knows whether the tide is up or down beyond the sea wall, and it is not only the romantics who admit that something has been lost,' said Kath.

At Burnham they stopped to pick up an extra 15 fathoms of anchor chain. When they dropped the buoy under power to continue, the engine cut out and *Sugar* was borne on a swift ebb towards the shiniest boat in Burnham, a Class 1 ocean racer launched the weekend before.

Mike put the tiller over and came up forward with the boathook. *Sugar* nosed past a stainless steel stanchion, and miraculously pushed her bowsprit over clear deckspace. He clung on, shoving and swearing, trying to disentangle her as neatly as she had managed to entangle herself and eventually secured her alongside with a line. Cramming fenders overboard, they nervously searched the 'gleaming aristocrat' for signs of trespass, but there was nothing out of place. Even the man who came out in a launch from the yard could find no evidence. They gave him names and addresses for good measure, and Mike managed to get the engine going again.

'Let's get out of this place,' he said, and steered a straight course for the fairway.

The engine saw them clear, but was making queer noises, and 'packed up for good' before they got to the mouth of the Roach. They decided to go up to Paglesham for the night, and give the children a run ashore.

'It's windy,' Mike said that night.

'Just as well we didn't go out,' Kath said as the children, tired from running up to the sweet shop and back, slept.

Paglesham. Frank Shuttlewood's old barge and yacht-building shed still stands against the sea wall

'What's wrong with the engine?'

'Don't ask me. We'll have to get someone to look at it in Whitstable.'

Whitstable was planned as the first stop so they could visit Peter and Joan Firmin who lived in Canterbury.

They remained windbound in Paglesham for the next five days. It was wild spring weather, a hot sun and great white clouds bowling over from the south-west. The grass rippled over the sea walls, the skylarks soared up and were swung away seawards. *Sugar Creek* snubbed on her anchor, and pitched about sickeningly for there is no shelter at Paglesham from the south-west, and even going ashore was a hazardous business with the children.

They tramped daily up to the village shop, grateful to be out of the wind between the high hedges that led away from the water; Shuttlewood's old boat-shed at the top of the hard was deserted, and there was nothing to do but lie on the lee side of the sea wall and wait.

'We're gypsies,' Mike said to the children. 'Collect some wood and we'll have a fire.'

'Lying there, wreathed in woodsmoke, it seemed a far cry from our brave cruise towards the West Country. It started to rain, and we all crawled under a dinghy. The children thought it all marvellous', Kath said.

On day five the weather forecast gave them Force 4 to 5, backing southerly. High water was at 0300 the following day.

'If we leave about six, that'll give us three hours to the Whitaker,' Mike said. 'That should do us nicely, and a southerly will serve after that.'

The evening was fair and the sunset calm and gold. The morning was grey, with a light, fair wind blowing. Kath started taking the lashings off the sails, and Mike went forward to haul up the anchor. The new gypsy wheel was the wrong size for the chain.

At every third link the chain jumped out. Getting the anchor in was an infuriating business, which took about twenty minutes, hammering the chain home over the ill-fitting gypsy with brute force. They were both sweating and swearing, with bruised fingers and a fixed hatred of all chandlers who got their specifications wrong.

'We'll listen to the Shipping Forecast,' Mike said, 'While we can still go back. Before we go out into the Crouch.'

It was south-westerly Force 4 or 5, backing southerly, Force 6, later.

'We'll be there by the time it blows up,' Mike said.

'And it's perfect now,' said Kath, which always seemed to her the main thing.

'I, who always hated crossing the estuary, with its arduous detour round the Foulness Sand, found I was longing to be out, and watched the Outer Crouch buoy swirl behind with a sense of great satisfaction. Usually it gave me a definite qualm, as marking the transition from safe river to dangerous sea, but now I was glad to see it go. The morning was grey and sharp; the buoys stood out clearly.'

'We'll have it dead on the nose once we're round the Whitaker,' Mike said.

The Whitaker was coming up fast, the beacon sticking up, apparently in the middle of nowhere, marking the end of the Foulness spit. The Crouch sailor, southward bound, aims to reach the Whitaker at dead low water, to carry the flood up the Swin. Kath stood with the leadline at the ready. There is no give in these sands. A boat hits them with a thud that brings the keel up into the soles of one's feet.

They were early and still pushing some ebb in the Swin. Mike knew that soon they would have the new flood with them, but the wind was freshening and he also knew that the weather going tide would make things a lot rougher.

"DID YOU CATCH THE FORECAST?"

Sugar Creek in Clements Green Creek, being prepared for her Atlantic crossing

Far away to the north a gleam of sun winked on Clacton Pier, and the horizon showed silver under the clouds. Southward the Kentish coast stood out plum blue and sharply cut, looking very near.

The clouds were scudding overhead and *Sugar* started to butt into the rising waves, too much canvas pressing her on. The children had gone quiet and pale and did not object to being put into their bunks. Kath did not feel like lingering below to keep them company. Much to her relief they went to sleep.

Mike was preparing to put a reef in when he suddenly shouted: 'Kath, come up here. Take the tiller!'

Mike frantically threw off the halyards. The gaff came down with a run, and they were enveloped in the flogging tan sail.

'Let her run off before the wind,' Mike said urgently, 'all the rigging's gone loose. The mast wasn't properly home in its step. It must have just dropped in. We could have been dismasted.'

Sugar Creek was jogging along comfortably under the staysail when suddenly a white light burst like a giant flower in the grey sky and a muffled report came on the wind.

'Whatever's that?'

Mike ran aft and shoved the helm over. 'It's for us – from the lightship – a warning.'

Sugar Creek lurched. The staysail flogged again and a heavy thud from below nearly flung them off their feet. The boat seemed to wallow; she lifted, and came down again with a crash that rattled the teeth.

'We're on the Barrow,' Mike said. 'Back the headsail.'

Kath stood at the tiller, cold with fright. She had never been aground in anything of a sea before, and the way the whole boat fell, jarring, off the lip of a wave, terrified her.

Sugar Creek thumped, and slewed about, and rolled with a great rattling of her lockers and bilges. The sea was yellow and breaking, very bleak and inhospitable, and away over the bows Kath could see the distant shape of the Barrow Lightship which had sent up the flare.

'She'll soon lift,' Mike said.

Sugar Creek continued to limp and bang on the shoal and Kath felt sick.

The boat rolled, touched and rolled again. The thick yellow sand stirred by the keel swirled off the rudder. Then she was rolling free, and the tiller was released from the East Barrow's grip. Mike eased the staysail sheets.

With Kath at the helm, Mike made a check of the chart, and told Kath to steer due east, before dispensing drinks to the girls – who were now crying – and told them to go back to sleep before tending to the rigging. After tightening the shrouds as best he could he re-set the main, but it was not up for long before it tore away from the gaff: all the sail slides had come adrift. Back under staysail alone, Kath stood in the cockpit 'watching the grey sea. There was nothing to be seen anywhere except the awkward, sliding waves: no ships, no land, no lightship, not even a buoy.' The sky

"BIT TOO CHOPPY FOR YOU CHAPS, WHAT?"

had darkened and the wind was strengthening. The boat pitched into the troughs and rode up the waves with a shouldering of spray over the bows, hung, rolled, and plunged off the next crest.

'See any buoys? The only thing we can do is run down to Harwich,' said Mike.

Kath huddled up on the bridgedeck 'as miserable as I'd ever felt in my life'.

Neither said anything. The mainsail was a write-off. Their only source of power was the headsail pulling them steadily over the tide.

Kath feeds Veronica and Hilary down below aboard *Sugar Creek*

All the time the wind was gradually strengthening.

At last on the port bow, a black cone revealed itself, it was the No 7 Barrow. 'Immediately our morale rose by several notches. Mike went below and checked up on the chart, and I watched it drop away astern at a satisfying speed. The tide was now under us. I longed for Harwich. The low grey cloud came lower, as ragged as the restless water, a grey drizzle shutting down on the distances.'

The children went to sleep. The afternoon dragged on and just on dusk they picked up the Mid-Gunfleet buoy and set course for the lit North-East Gunfleet. As it grew dark the rain cleared but the wind did not let up. On the tops of the waves they could see the lights of Harwich twinkling on the port bow. Mike watched them and said nothing.

'The children were miserable but not complaining, resigned in a way that made me feel worse than if they had held this uncomfortable journey against us,' Kath recalled.

'Are we nearly there?'

'Yes, you can see the lights now,' she said encouragingly.

She lit the Primus to heat up some soup, while being seasick in a bucket wedged against the galley while struggling with the tin opener. Then a locker door burst open, throwing half its contents onto the cabin sole. The Tilley lamp swung 'mutinously' against its moorings, and the jerking light flared round the cabin.

She tried to empty the soup into the saucepan but half of it went over the galley and slipped across the Formica in a gluey stream. She looked at it and was sick again.

'I want some pop,' Veronica said.

Sugar Creek would not point up for Harwich under staysail alone with wind and tide on her beam.

'But we're not in any danger,' Mike said, 'The boat's taking it beautifully. She's riding it like an old duck.' There was a measure of satisfaction in his voice.

'But the children...and besides if we miss Harwich, there's nowhere else. Where do we land up?'

'Well, at this rate it will be Norway,' joked Mike. 'The only thing I'm worried about – it's lowish water now, and, we're off our chart.'

They had by now wallowed past Harwich and were near the Cutler Shoal off Bawdsey.

A pilot boat was rolling into Harwich.

'Can't I flash her up?' asked Kath.

'Oh, heavens, no,' Mike said, rather irritably.

Veronica was being sick, and wanting a drink, incessantly. Mike considered anchoring.

'In this? Oh, please no, it would be dreadful.'

It was now 2000, they had been under way 16 hours and there was no sign of the wind easing up.

'There's a ship,' Mike said at last.

Kath had learnt Morse in the Guides, long ago, and used a torch to signal SOS.

'With every flash went a telepathic message from my heart so powerful that I felt sure it must pierce the captain as he stood on his bridge.'

'She's altering course,' Mike said.

'She isn't.'

'She is.'

A red light joined the starboard green as the railway ferry *Suffolk* approached and made a lee for *Sugar Creek* now under bare poles.

The ferry had a big fender, wide enough to walk along, all round her topside. Just above it, an amidships door was open and some men were framed in its light. From the deck above, some one flung down a rope. *Sugar Creek*'s crosstrees were carried away by the *Suffolk*'s fender. She rolled, rose up on the swell and the same fender came down hard on her bulwarks, stoving them in with a crashing and tearing of timber.

Kath handed the children out of the hatch and saw them lifted up towards the square of light, where a man in a string vest was leaning down with his arms outstretched. As *Sugar* rolled up he grasped first one, passing her back inside, then – on the next roll – the second. Next Kath scrambled up after the children as *Sugar Creek* made an 'awful grinding of against the steel ship'.

'The children were being carried away by two burly sailors through what

Rescued by a North Sea Ferry

appeared to be a railway siding. Stumbling over the railway lines I ran after them like a ewe deprived of its lambs, and with no more intelligent thought in my head than just that,' Kath recalled. 'The train shed seemed a most odd place to be in. But the solidity of it charmed me. In a minute we were up some steps and in a fuggy saloon surrounded by curious, friendly stewards offering pint mugs of tea. The children were thrilled.'

'We've been shipwrecked, like Rupert Bear,' Hilary said, with intense satisfaction. A steward gave her an apple 'as big as a grapefruit'.

Sugar Creek had started a plank and was making water, and Mike had been told to abandon her. She was now on a tow astern. But the towline soon parted. *Sugar* was left to her fate, rolling in the midnight sea astern, reported over the radio to Trinity House as 'a danger to shipping'.

They were met at Harwich by the police and a marine insurance agent and were then driven to the Pier Hotel, where they were given a room for four.

'The hotel was the final bliss, with bedside lamps that popped on and off, and a view over the river with the light buoys splashing the wild, black water. We stood and regarded the view with very different feelings from the children who were thrilled. We seemed to have failed so abysmally that it did not seem that there was any more to say. Everybody being so kind seemed to make it worse,' said Kath.

Veronica recalled it differently. She told me: 'When it happened I remember mother being very cool headed. And Hilary and I loved it. We got to stay in this luxurious hotel and we were in the newspapers. Our school friends read that we'd been shipwrecked...they were well impressed.'

The next morning they took the children down on the beach early, while they considered the events of the night before. Hilary and Veronica rattled the shells in their buckets, eager for breakfast in 'the posh hotel'.

Chastened by their experience the Peytons were mollified to discover that they were not the only sailors in trouble in the Thames Estuary that night. The lifeboat had tended two other yachts: *Petasus* and *St Barbara*. The first was aground on the Sunk Sand, the second had been dismasted. Both had been competing in the RORC Southsea – Harwich Race.

'One thing we've learned,' Kath said, 'and that's how nice everyone can be when you're in trouble'.

'Look,' said Mike.

Coming round Landguard Point was the Trinity House Vessel *Triton*, with *Sugar Creek* on a long tow behind her. She was low in the water as part of her decks had been stove in by the ferry and she had taken on a lot of water. They headed back to the hotel for breakfast and Kath remembers being dressed in paint-spattered jeans with her toes poking out of worn deck shoes: there had been no time for packing the night before. Halfway through their bacon and eggs, the skipper of the *Triton* appeared and asked, 'Are you the survivors?'

The description gave them a jolt. Mike went off to sort out the boat and Kath and the children returned home.

Sugar Creek was towed up to Walton Backwaters where she lay in one of the mudberths off Wyatt's yard. All down one side the bulwarks and covering board was stove in, guardrails buckled and dangling. The cross-trees had gone, shrouds and rigging swung in the breeze. Below she was a shambles of broken, mud-slimed gear. For weeks the bilges gave up the odd rasher of bacon, a rusty fork. The ship's papers, in copper-plate Norwegian, were all in a pulp, fit only for the dustbin.

The insurance paid for the repairs, which took three months, and also the salvage claim from the Trinity House tender.

'Immediately after the accident, I vowed I would never, in any circumstances, set foot on board a boat again, and I really believed that I meant it this time – it was certainly not the first time I had said it,' Kath recalled.

But as she went over and over the events of that wild night in the estuary, she came to the conclusion that the boat had not failed them. 'It was ourselves that had not been equal to the occasion.

'It is not the same thing at all to discuss it, warm and comfortable round a fire, with a glass of something, as it is to be doing it, cold and sick and frightened to death. The sea is very frightening. I will never change my opinion about that.'

Nevertheless three months later Kath was back aboard: 'It was then that I found out our mishap off Harwich had certainly left its mark on me'.

"IT'LL BE GOOD TO GET IN, TIE UP AND RELAX"

• 12 •

The Solent

It was time to give the Solent a go.

In August Mike sailed the boat out of Walton Backwaters, still then, the Secret Waters of Arthur Ransome fame, to Lymington, with John Barstow and another crewman. There, Kath and the children joined him for a fortnight's holiday, as the delivery crew returned to Essex. The plan was to potter about the Solent to build up Kath's confidence again. There would be beaches for the children, and sheltered water while Kath could lie on the deck and Mike busy himself with jobs. They had never sailed in the Solent before, and Mike showed his wife the chart, with harbours and snug little anchorages dotted everywhere, no more than a few miles apart. 'There's always somewhere to run to, whatever happens. You don't have to go to Norway,' he joked. 'Dead easy.'

All the same, when they left Lymington the following morning, bound for Yarmouth, 4 miles away on the Isle of Wight, Kath went below and lay on her bunk. 'I could feel myself trembling all over. It seems ridiculous in retrospect, but I was scared stiff by the whole holiday, from Lymington to Yarmouth, to Newtown, to Cowes and back to Beaulieu, where we left *Sugar* ten days later. Even the Solent's undoubted charm did nothing to allay my anxiety; indeed, I loved every little harbour dearly and only wished I never need leave it to seek another.' The weather did not help, for it blew hard including the day they left Newtown for Cowes when a gale was forecast from the south. The Solent was grey and cold, the shore inhospitable.

'We'll be there in less than an hour,' Mike said, 'It's only 5 miles. Besides, Jack is coming down to join us there in the morning so we've got to go.' Jack Worsley was another Clements Green Creeker coming to help Mike sail her home.

'That at least meant I could lie on my bunk and be frightened in peace. I watched the bleak water scud past, and the grey clouds coming lower. "Suppose we can't get into Cowes?," Kath said.'

'With a southerly we can go into Southampton Water,' Mike said, 'but we will get into Cowes. The engine's working now.'

He started it, to prove his point. All the same, with the southerly behaving as forecast, to manoeuvre on to the visitors' piles in Cowes was no easy matter. They had never been into Cowes before and there seemed to be a lot of shiny boats to miss. The glossy flanks of the varnished *Drumbeat* slipping past and the immaculate monster *Stormvogel* lying on the piles beyond, gave Kath the trembles again.

'Who shall we go alongside?' Mike wondered, somewhat urgently, for furious gusts were sweeping the river, and *Sugar*'s tiny engine was having difficulty in holding her on course.

'Not *Stormvogol*, for heaven's sake,' Kath muttered.

A motor-sailer lay downstream of *Stormvogel*, with people on deck. Mike bawled at them, 'Can I come alongside?' and they made welcoming gestures back. They went round again, the engine running on full throttle. Mike, always distrustful of engines, had only a single lashing on the sails, so he could set them at short notice. But the engine did not fail and they arrived alongside with all their motley fenders out. 'As our line was taken, I felt about ten years younger in an instant.'

However, they were not to rest in peace. The skipper of the motor-sailer was a woman, and she had her own

Veronica and Hilary aboard *Sugar Creek*

very definite ideas of how a boat should be moored up alongside. As she had been so helpful in welcoming them alongside they were quite happy to go along with her. Mike rowed out warps where she directed, until '*Sugar Creek* was like a cat's cradle, trussed uneasily in springs, stern-lines and bowlines so that one could scarcely put a foot on deck'.

'We don't do it like this on the East Coast,' Mike, slightly peeved, told his counterpart. 'Thank the stars,' he added under his breath.

They sat below listening to the restless grinding of fenders, and the occasional jar. The crew of the motor-sailer paced anxiously round their deck. When Mike stuck his head out of the companionway the skipper of the motor-sailer said: 'Why don't you go up to the Folly Inn? It's far more sheltered up there. You'll be far more comfortable.'

'We're all right here,' Mike said shortly.

Kath felt very embarrassed, especially as the woman, still pacing her decks, started ejaculating, "My God I can't stand it," at intervals. Kath muttered to Mike: 'Do you think we ought to go?'

'She can go if she wants. I bet her engine is six times the size of ours.'

Kath looked down the trots; most of the piles were holding three or more boats, and there was no obvious close place for them to move to. The woman suggested several more times that they should try the Folly, in spite of Mike explaining to her their shortage of engine power. The battle of wills continued until the motor-sailer skipper said: 'You're a bloody nuisance. If you're not going, I am.' She mustered her two male crew from below and the Peytons stood by to await orders.

Disentangling her boat from its web of mooring warps was an operation which took about an hour. Kath completely lost track of which rope was doing what, awaiting her orders to pull, undo, pass over, under, through, round...At one point the woman shouted at her, "Your knot is unwending".

'It's unwhat?' Kath said to Mike.

'Coming undone.'

'I thought that was the whole idea.' Having started by trying to be helpful, Kath became angry, and then giggly when at last with a burst of engine power that, as Mike had prophesied, would have done credit to the *Queen Mary*, her boat leapt out from its bonds and Kath felt that there was a lot to be said for the East Coast isolation on the end of an anchor chain.

But Mike was now absorbing material for South Coast cartoons and the Solent was then as it is now the Mecca of UK yachting.

The motor-sailer's departure left them alongside *Myth of Malham*. As *Sugar Creek* surged, one of her springs pulled a cleat off her neighbour's deck. But when her owner, the top racing skipper and designer John Illingworth, he turned up to see how she was in the early hours of the morning, he was friendly and unconcerned. 'Better to find out the fixing is no good in harbour than out at sea,' was all he said.

'He restored my shaken faith in all-knowing Solent sailors,' said Kath.

Jack joined them the following day. Jack was a commercial artist from London's Maida Vale, tall and quiet and amusing. He had a thick grey beard, which gave him an imposing appearance, but underneath he was 'as kind and as soft as butter'. The children adored him, and he would tell them stories for hours, and sing Carmen to them. When they set sail for Lymington the following morning Jack amused the girls by pulling his head below his polo neck jumper, and scrubbed the deck as a headless man.

'Yachts beat past us more under water than on top, yellow oilskins gleaming in the sunshine. I was miserable again, the whole holiday having proved to me that visions of basking in hot sun on an idle deck were mere figments of magazine advertisements.' As *Sugar Creek* made her wide gaffer's tacks doggedly into the eye of the wind, the sleek Cowes yachts pitched past them, pointing up, porpoising with a convex flash of white boot-topping in clouds of flying spray.

'Ugh, how wet,' Kath said, 'At least on *Sugar Creek*, we can sit in the cockpit without getting soaked.'

But trying to make Mike feel better about his boat's laggardly progress failed miserably.

'They're getting there, which is more than we are,' he said.

When the tide turned against them there was still a several mile beat to Lymington, and therefore they decided on Beaulieu instead.

'Well, of course, you meant to all along, didn't you?' Jack said happily.

'Oh, yes, of course. After all, we've done Lymington.'

As the trees of the New Forest closed round them shutting out the wind, Kath's spirits lifted considerably. At Buckler's Hard, the cluster of masts, limp burgees, and ponies grazing at the water's edge greeted them.

They moored to the pontoon and a woman on the next boat said to Kath:

'What's it like outside?'

'Horrible.'

When she went below Mike was annoyed. 'I hadn't displayed the required sangfroid. Another yacht came in just ahead of us and the woman asked her question again. The young man at the halyards, streaming water from head to foot, replied cheerily, "Oh, all right. Rather choppy."'

Kath's feeling of inadequacy among the Solent milieu eased when a yacht ahead

cast off and fouled another boat's boom under her back-stay, breaking it in half. 'Appalled at the results of this simple accident, we watched the guilty yacht return to face the consequences and, like everybody else on the moorings, pretending not to, surreptitiously eavesdropped on the ensuing conversation. It was civilized in the extreme, not an angry word disturbed the afternoon, merely a discussion on insurance claims and exchange of addresses. We were very impressed.'

Later on Kath was all but knocked off her feet by an almighty crash aft. 'I shot up the hatchway to find that we had been rammed broadside on by a boat trying to come alongside under full throttle and with the tide under him.' The errant yacht was completely undamaged, but her metal stem had fractured one of *Sugar's* 4 x 4 inch frames where it came above the deck to support the bulwarks.

'Take my lines. Take my lines,' her skipper shouted, hurling warps across the now widening stretch of water between the two boats. 'Look at that!' Mike moaned when he saw the cracked frame.

'When the man came alongside again he was tactless enough to remark that it was "only a block of wood".'

'The whole bloody boat's only a block of wood,' Mike told him.

'Mike was not nearly as polite as our neighbours had been over the broken boom, and afterwards I pointed this out to him to get my own back,' Kath said. 'You should have offered him a drink and said, "By the way, old boy, what's the name of your insurance man?"' Kath disassociated herself from the unpleasantness and took the children ashore for a walk in the woods.

The North Sea rescue still played on Kath's mind so when Mike decided he wanted to take the next progressive step in his sailing career – to cross the Bay of Biscay –

Kath was not prepared to take the children and stayed behind in Essex, listening to the Shipping Forecast and making her own DRs on an atlas. Jack Worsley and John Barstow, and a friend of John's called Riq, joined Mike so that *Sugar Creek* could be sailed with two men on watch and two off for the passage. The destination was San Sebastian in the Basque country. This was because 'If you turn left at Ushant and keep going long enough you will see a coastline going either north and south, or east and west. If the former you turn south, and if the latter you turn east, and San Sebastian will appear.' To back up this rule of thumb, Mike had been taking navigation lessons twice nightly for some weeks. The combination worked as six days after leaving Lymington without any sight of land after Ushant, San Sebastian appeared right on the bowsprit out of an early morning mist, just when he was thinking that, according to his dead reckoning, he would shortly be running aground.

To celebrate the longest passage any of them had ever made the four men ordered the best meal a local restaurateur could provide. But when it turned up it 'looked like pieces of sago pudding in whitewash'. Only Mike could stomach the local speciality: hake's brain. But it was not as good as stewed Alsatian. On the passage home they called at Lorient, to inspect German U-Boat pens and Guilvinec where they overslept and, having rounded Pointe de Penmarc'h, were fog-bound within half an hour's sail of the Raz du Seine. They now turned back south and stemmed their fair tide until the fog lifted. By the time it did they had lost the tidal lift and had to tack westwards to clear the Île de Sein. 'Our sleepy indulgence cost us dear,' said Mike, 'as all that night and the next day we were becalmed within sight and sound of the whistle buoy which marks the end of the Chauses de Seine.'

When the wind came they had a good stiff two reef breeze to round Ushant with, and called at St Peter Port, Guernsey, before coming up Channel 'in three tacks': from Cherbourg across to Beachy Head, from there to Boulogne, and from Boulogne to Dover.

Some warm weather sailing in the Thames Estuary and one particular unforgettable night cruise to Whitstable to make that missed rendezvous with Peter and Joan Firmin, restored Kath's faith in sailing, especially as John and Jack now sailed as permanent crew. So that the following summer when the opportunity came to leave the children with Kath's mother for a week, she was happy at the prospect of going to France again, with John and Jack as crew. She joined the boat at Lymington, but by the time they had reached the Needles she felt sick and went below. 'I felt that, compared to being sick and still having to carry on being useful, being sick in peace was pure luxury.'

Sugar Creek reached into the darkness, crashing eagerly into the Channel. The wind was north westerly, Force 6, the sea 'full of holes, the night dark'. Kath lay braced in her bunk 'miserable with fear, and trembling like a leaf'. She was no longer afraid the boat would capsize, 'but I had a long way, still, to go to accept that there was no danger in a passage like this,' said the author whose imagination had by now produced five published novels. 'The roar of the water a few inches from my ears, the occasional crash and whip of sheets and blocks on the deck above my head and the shuddering crashes as the bows dropped from the top of a bigger wave than usual into the trough below all kept me shivering and sweating with funk, my face buried in the damp pillow.' By dawn the wind eased, and Cherbourg's great walls put their protective arms around the little boat. A high façade of old grey, very French

PEYTON

buildings stared silently down across a cobbled road. They made a reconnaissance down the rows of silent, dew-wet yachts and went alongside a green English sloop moored up to a fishing boat. No sooner had they rowed out their lines and sat down to a cup of tea than they were hailed. 'I put my head out and found a humourless face regarding me from our neighbour. "Your fenders are squeaking," he said.'

When he received the news, Mike said: 'He can take them off if he likes.'

They decided to shift berths and when a drowsy solo sailor came in at the helm of a humble Silhouette, they made him welcome, took his lines and offered him tea. Having had such a cold welcome themselves, and finding it an unpleasant ending to a successful passage, they felt especially keen to make it otherwise for the only other sign of life in the harbour. The skipper had come across from Christchurch and fell asleep over the tea, relaxed in the knowledge he was among friends. It was a stoic trip considering the conditions.

The wind went east and fell off, and the temperature soared which delighted Kath who now looked forward to drinking vin ordinaire and eating grapes on deck rather than facing a slow and frustrating passage across the Baie de la Seine. Unfortunately, such was the skipper's disposition, that wherever they happened to be lounging, a tin of varnish and brush would be pushed conveniently to hand, along with a few sheets of sandpaper.

PEYTON

"BUT IT'S YOUR FAVOURITE, MACARONI CHEESE"

'Why is it?' Kath continued, 'that, whatever harbour we are in, there are always hammering noises or sawing noises coming from *Sugar Creek*. And do you *have* to wear a boiler suit?' You can take the man out of Clements Green Creek...

One of the yachting magazines was at this time running a correspondence concerning the poor sartorial image displayed by the average British yachtsman ashore: there was a letter from a man who said that whenever he went on a cruise, he not only carried a casual reefer jacket, pressed flannels, and evening dress, but hunting breeches and boots in case he came upon the opportunity to ride a horse. Kath, who preferred land horses to sea horses, took some delight in pointing it out to her husband. Kath's kind of horse-riding, however, was similar to Mike's kind of sailing: she did not like show-jumping, which could be compared to racing, but hacking, which is like cruising: 'just going along watching the passing countryside and enjoying it'.

After the liner *Queen Mary* called in to pick up cruise passengers, the more humble cruisers aboard *Sugar Creek* left to head back to the Solent.

In a light easterly breeze Kath lay on deck listening to *Gardener's Question Time* on the transistor radio. Jack was at the tiller, his legs draped over the cockpit coamings.

'Ship ahoy,' John said, opening one eye from his sunbathing.

'Miles away,' said Kath.

They were in mid-Channel, and *Sugar Creek* was little more than drifting, her sails just filled.

'What do you think, Mike?' Jack called down the hatch.

Mike looked out. 'Oh, he'll alter in a minute and go astern of us.'

The sun shone brightly; *Sugar* rolled on the swell, and her sails collapsed, and filled again.

The ship still did not alter course. She came on inexorably, growing larger very quickly. Mike came up on deck and watched her with a frown.

Kath felt herself getting nervous. 'Can't you start the engine?' she said.

'He must see us,' Mike said.

'By the time we get that thing going...' John said, shrugging. *Sugar*'s engine had to be primed, and the heavy flywheel swung several times to get it started. And the ship was close now, a trim Dutchman, the sun shining on her upperworks. She was coming straight towards them, throwing up a curling bow-wave. They all sat watching, not saying anything, not even doing anything useful, like pulling on lifejackets.

'I watched, and saw the great flaring vee of the ship's stem and the white foam shooting out ahead of it. It was such a horrid sight I turned my back on it, and went on sitting on the coamings looking out on the calm, sunshot sea on the other side, thinking of my girls,' Kath said.

Mike said to Jack, 'Go about'.

'Surely it's too late?' he replied.

With her back to the ship Kath heard the heavy thumping of the ship's engine, and smelt the hot reek of diesel. Jack did not put the helm over, and Mike said no more.

'The next moment, *Sugar Creek* gave a great lurch and her stern went up in the air as if lifted by a hand from under the sea. I heard our Sunday dinner hissing over on to the flames, there was a great crashing of spars and sails and blocks being flung everywhere, and then we were coasting down the side of a shining wave. I turned round and saw the great bows hiss past our stern.'

The name of the steamer, in case they forgot it, was spelled out in big letters right over their heads: *Ladon Amsterdam*. The sun shone brightly on the bridge, which was empty, there was nobody on the foredeck, but on the stern two men were running from one side to the other staring into the wake.

Having faced the situation with 'ludicrous British phlegm', the crew of *Sugar Creek* now reacted violently. John and Michael danced on the deck waving their fists and swearing after the departing stern; Kath burst into tears and Jack shifted his hand on the tiller, tugged his beard in disbelief and said, 'God bless my soul'. Bill Sowerbutts was still talking about compost. The dinner was all over the galley. 'Bloody Dutchman' said Mike, writing the name of the ship no-one would ever forget in the log. Still muttering, he went below to salvage the dinner.

Next morning's fog dressed *Sugar Creek*'s sails with dew as Kath came on watch to witness the upperworks of a ship moving with her hull hidden in the blanket of mist. This one was not so close. Eventually a whiter patch in the fog steadily pieced itself together into Old Harry Rocks.

· 13 ·

Lost at Sea

As so often happens with newcomers to sailing who grow into handy, reliable crew, John Barstow wanted to exercise the skills he'd discovered aboard *Sugar Creek* as skipper of his own craft. It was 1963. He sold his van and bought *Snipe*, a double-ended 18 ft gaff cutter built in the latter part of Queen Victoria's reign. She was once owned by the founder of the Fambridge Yacht Club, Francis B Cooke, who first laid eyes on her in 1897 as she beat through the anchorage 'her lee decks just awash...sailing fast and staying with the precision of clockwork'. Even though 'her foredeck was running with water', Cooke coveted her from that day on and two years later bought her and for three years from 1899 cruised extensively on the East Coast. She had a tiny cabin with no room for a galley: cooking was done in the cockpit on a Primus stove. Her 'headroom' was described enthusiastically by a crewman of Cooke's who exclaimed: 'Golly, what a ship! Why look, skipper, I can sit up with my hat on'. That this was said without irony gives some idea of the confinement expected in yachts a century ago. In his last season in her, Cooke, in his book *Pocket Cruisers*, describes an Easter gale at Fambridge when: 'Yacht after yacht began to drag, for in those days the moorings were not of the best. Owners seemed to think that anything would hold their boat so long as it was fairly heavy, and used for the purpose such things as bits of condemned agricultural implements and old bedsteads. I counted no fewer than nine yachts dragging their ground tackle at one and the same time.'

In Mike's time the moorings had improved, though there were still some using old tractor wheels filled with concrete to anchor their craft to the river bed.

John bought *Snipe* from his old friend Gordon Hamilton.

April was doing its best to live up to its name of being the cruellest month when I arrived at Titchmarsh Marina in the Walton Backwaters, Essex where Gordon Hamilton's 24 ft clinker-built Finesse, *Bramble* is moored. The daffodils surrounding the marina's grassy banks were having their yellow trumpets tweaked by an icy north-east wind and the new high sun was hidden in bitter grey cloud coming in off the North Sea. Gordon was wearing the normal uniform: royal blue boiler suit and Breton fisherman's cap as he invited me aboard through an oversized wheelhouse he has built on top of his tiny home. Inside the wheelhouse I sat listening as Gordon, 76, recounted his 50 years of sailing which began in 1958 when he read Weston Martyr's *£200 Millionaire*, the book about Corinthian sailing in cheap boats. 'It's my bible,' said the ruddy-faced former engineering company director as he stretched out his legs and fitted his feet into a pair of tartan slippers. He was keen to tell me every last detail of the 29 boats he has owned: from a Pintail Major, through a Folkboat, Debutante, Hillyard, Vertue. When I tried gently to move him onto *Snipe*, he said "I'm coming to that."

Snipe was lying in Ramsgate harbour, very forlorn – since Gordon had lost interest in her as he now owned a bigger boat, a plywood Debutante, *Misty* – and obviously in need of a major refit. John decided to make her seaworthy enough just to get her back to Fambridge where the real work could begin. Jack Worsley agreed to help him, so the two of them defected to Kent, and spent each weekend working on the little cutter.

Gordon Hamilton

They took out all the ballast to examine the hull, and cleaned out the bilges. She needed a new mast and John bought a pine pole from a Canterbury firm which built cherry-picking ladders for Kent's fruit orchards. Jack, who was a meticulous carpenter, planed it down to the required dimensions. The weekend for *Snipe*'s return to her ancestral home was fixed, and Mike agreed to sail *Sugar Creek* over to Ramsgate on the Friday night, in order to sail in company with his old shipmate back to Fambridge.

Mike's crew included John Young and Tom Bolton, the proud owner of the lifeboat which had nearly caused havoc off Burnham several years before. He now owned a 120-year-old 40 ft smack, *Maria*, which he had dug out of the mud at Tollesbury and was 're-fitting'. This entailed the removal of 10 gallons' worth of live eels from her bilges and getting her towed home to Clements Green Creek.

Kath, at this time, was writing her ninth novel, *The Maplin Bird*, about fugitives on the run from the law who use a Southend smack to make a getaway only to be forced into Ramsgate in bad weather. So, leaving the children with her mother, she too, joined *Sugar Creek* to do some research on the port.

Kath was on the helm, as they sailed down the Crouch, and put *Sugar* ashore off Wallasea Bay, while dreamily imagining herself to be one of the novel's characters, Emily, the heroine of the piece.

'As the tiller stiffened under my hand, no fictional character could have felt more horror than I did. Mike was up like a shot from below hissing "Kath" with a controlled venom that froze the feeble excuses I was trying to utter.' It was half ebb and the prospect of not getting off was desperate: the total ruin of a carefully-planned weekend's work. Mike set about starting the engine, while the others let go the sheets and prodded experimentally with the boathook. The wind had been light and they had not gone on with any great force; with the engine in reverse, flat out, the old boat 'shuddered out of the mud, churning up turgid black eddies off the slackening rudder'. Kath went below to her bunk, 'too ashamed to want to talk about it, furiously angry and indignant and fed-up'.

Daylight saw them reefed down in the Swin with a north-easterly Force 5 pushing them easily to Ramsgate where they arrived at midday.

The boisterous wind and hot sunshine made a perfect combination, bringing out the trippers and the beach brigade and the holiday atmosphere. John and Jack were working on the mast on the quayside and were asked to join *Sugar Creek*'s crew for fish and chips. 'No time,' said John. 'No money,' said Jack, pushing his hand through a hole in his pocket and waving it at the hungry arrivals. Kath wandered around the port beneath its peculiar pink brick arches which held back the chalk cliffs from tumbling into the harbour and weaved away at her plot. When she arrived back at the dock *Snipe*'s mast was being lowered over the quayside into its place on the deck below, very nearly putting paid to the Corporation of Ramsgate's fairy-lighting programme in the process, when the fittings at the top got hung up in the power lines. Six pairs of hands set up the standing and running rigging, bent on the sails and coiled down. *Snipe* locked out of the inner harbour and rafted up to *Sugar Creek* alongside the massive stone arm of the southern pier. The boats rolled gently in the Ramsgate swell, fenders creaking, warps dipping, and stretching.

'A late bus ground up the hill. I heard the gear-change, and thought of the shining expanse of Pegwell Bay beneath the headlights, where I had decided my hero would sail for the last time before going to prison on a charge of smuggling. His boat was based on *Snipe*. We had always admired *Snipe* and were pleased that she was staying in the family.'

John was too excited to sleep, and sat in the cockpit, his face caught every now and then by the restless illuminations from the inner harbour which his mast had almost felled.

At 0130 *Sugar Creek* slipped her warps from the giant cast iron bollards of Ramsgate's stone pier and motored out of the harbour, towing *Snipe*, and there was a discussion as to which of *Sugar*'s crew was to transfer to *Snipe*, so Tom and John Young cut cards and Tom won. Mike cast *Snipe* off and hoisted sail. The south-westerly wind was light in the lee of the land. The two skippers had agreed to rendezvous at Whitstable.

By the loom of the North Foreland lighthouse the crew of *Sugar Creek* watched the three on board *Snipe* sorting out some teething troubles with the sails; and put alongside once to pass over a spare foresail which was rigged as a bermudian mainsail, and *Snipe* immediately started to pull ahead of *Sugar Creek*.

Her crew jeered, and in the darkness all they could see was her receding port light, and the glow of the Tilley lamp from her hatchway. Kath turned in.

Once round the Foreland, *Sugar Creek* and *Snipe* faced a dead beat through the Gore Channel to Whitstable.

Kath woke up to hear some shouting, it was the crew of *Snipe* jeering again. She asked Mike what was going on.

'We can't keep up with her. They say they're tired of waiting for us.'

Snipe still 'sailed fast and stayed like clockwork'.

'See you in Whitstable, slowcoach,' John shouted triumphantly across the water. 'We can't hang about all night.'

Faintly in the darkness they could make out *Snipe*'s shape inshore of *Sugar Creek*, the gleam of phosphorescence at her bows.

Snipe

'She was travelling like the little thoroughbred she was, John on her foredeck, laughing as they hardened in sheets and went away from us. The wind was freshening. I saw the glow of John's cigarette for a moment, and then just the darkness. I went back to bed. That was the last we ever saw of them.'

Sugar Creek made very slow progress in the moderate headwind, and was still east of Herne Bay pier when the tide turned at 0900. It was a grey, miserable day, and the wind freshened steadily to a Force 6.

'It's no good trying to make anything against the tide, Mike said. 'We might as well anchor and wait for the flood.'

Sugar's engine would not move her against the tide and a headwind of that force. So they laid out the full scope of her chain downstream of the pier, and she took up hard and lay quietly.

'*Snipe* must have got in hours ago. How they'll scoff.'

Even with the help of her engine, *Sugar* had been unable to keep pace with *Snipe*. Kath could picture John's satisfaction, going away from *Sugar Creek* with such ease.

'I'm surprised we didn't see her when it got light, the visibility wasn't bad.'

'If she was inshore of us, it's not easy to see a boat against the coastline.'

They sat around talking, eating, and doing the odd jobs that came to hand, cleaning the Primuses, and putting more coal on the stove. Whitstable is a drying harbour, so even when the tide turned there was no hurry, for they could only get in at high water. It was dusk by the time *Sugar's* bowsprit eventually poked into the tiny basin, and they did not expect to see the others greet them at such a late hour. But they did expect to see *Snipe*.

'There she is,' John Young said, 'Up in the corner.'

Kath went ashore and walked round the harbour wall. The boat in the corner was a modern cruiser. 'I looked at every boat and Whitstable harbour is very small; *Snipe* wasn't there. I went back and reported.'

Sugar Creek's crew were catching the train home, but Mike and Kath were staying aboard. They were not particularly worried; if anything had gone wrong, the wind was fair to run back to Ramsgate. 'They must be in either Margate or Ramsgate,' Mike said. 'We'll check with the Harbour Master.'

The Harbour Master's office was empty. They waited around, trying to convince themselves they weren't worried. They were both aware, although neither mentioned it, that *Snipe* had not been towing a dinghy, nor did she have any flares on board. *Sugar Creek* had a full complement of flares, red and white, and both Mike and Kath had thought of offering John a few when we towed *Snipe* out of harbour, 'But we had both rejected the idea as psychologically depressing! How wrong we were, to have been so ridiculously tactful, was now about to be proved.'

Eventually a figure appeared in the Harbour Master's office. Its occupant said: 'Well, I'm not in charge I'm just standing in', grumbling in the way of all commercial harbour officials when bothered by yachtsmen, but he did reach for the telephone.

'We'll try Ramsgate and Margate.' They stood looking at the dusty old pictures of barges and the tide-tables and calendars and charts, listening to the conversation. *Snipe* was not in Ramsgate or Margate.

'We'll try the Reculver Coastguards – see if they saw her go by.'

The Reculver Coastguards recited descriptions of every sailing boat that had passed them that day.

'There weren't very many but our ears pricked up when the man repeated "Gaff cutter, tan sails, eight am." Then Mike shook his head and said, 'That was us. She was rigged bermudian.' *Snipe* had not passed Reculver.

'It's no good searching until daylight,' the official said, 'as soon as it's light the lifeboat will launch, and Manston will send a helicopter.'

The wind swept round the corners of the warehouses and out in the darkness slicked the fast-running ebb down over the estuary shoals. It was out of their hands. They went back on board and turned in.

In the morning the search was put into operation.

Mike went to London for his day at *The New Scientist*. Kath went home to collect the children.

Gordon, who had sold the boat to his old friend, lived in Ramsgate and was contacted by the police and asked to keep in touch in order to identify anything that might be found. 'I had been out sailing that night myself,' he told me, 'and I remember a gust putting *Misty* over on her side off Hollowshore.'

That same night an angler fishing off the stone causeway at Broadstairs noticed a set of sails and a mast drifting by and reported his findings to police.

Kath arrived at Long Acre just minutes before Mike phoned.

'They've just rung me to say a fisherman has brought in Jack's body. I think you'd better go and tell Pat what has happened.'

Pat was Tom Bolton's wife, who lived up the lane.

'The police are getting in touch with John's parents.'

'*Snipe*'s black hull was found in two halves, keel-less. The bodies of John, 28, and Tom, 40, were never recovered. The body of Jack, 45, had been picked up off the North Foreland. Gordon went to identify him at Broadstairs mortuary. 'He was complete in his oilskins and his hands were cupped as though he had been hanging onto something,' he told me. It had been a busy night for the lifeboats at both Ramsgate and Margate. A motor-boat had run aground on the Margate Hook Sand and her crew burned clothing as a flare. And, mysteriously, an inflatable dinghy had been found moored to a buoy off the North Foreland with a dead body in it. This was the late summer of 1963 and The Great Train Robbery had taken place just weeks before and there had been some reports of suitcases being carried aboard a motor-boat at Ramsgate, where *Snipe*'s broken hull now lay. The Ramsgate lifeboat mechanic, Bob Cannon, and Gordon speculated about these incidents and whether they were linked in some way. But John Ray, an ex-lifeboatman himself, and now a spokesman for the very busy Ramsgate boat, the coxswain of which is Ian Cannon, Bob's grandson, told me that local boatmen were only too happy to substantiate the mysterious rumours as 'Fleet Street were paying well to have their reporters taken out on boats'.

Mike later wondered if he might have heard something had they not been under power, and so been able to go to their assistance.

Snipe was old, but she had been well cared for most of her life. Gordon had sailed her abroad several times the previous year, and had removed her mast during the winter and fitted in its place a coal-stove chimney. A crew had once left his wet trousers draped near the stove – a Caledonian Dumpy – while they went ashore. When they returned they found the trousers scorched as were two pieces of plywood that Gordon had used as shields to protect the bunksides. But there was no structural damage.

Opinions aired at the inquest concurred: that she had gone on the Margate Sand, and pounded until she broke up. She had been travelling fast when they last saw her, and the impact would have been considerable.

There were no flares or lifejackets aboard *Snipe* and she had no dinghy. John was short of money at the time and was about to spend the whole winter equipping her with the necessary gear. 'The whole point of our going to Ramsgate was to escort him across the estuary for the sake of safety, and the fact that we sailed in the dark, and therefore could not see him when he needed help, was dictated by the fact that there was only the weekend at our disposal, and that gaff-cutters, one engineless and one underpowered, are forced to sail according to the tide, not the hours of daylight,' Kath said. They had already abandoned the idea of going straight across to the Crouch, and in the circumstances the passage to Whitstable was a modest enough undertaking, certainly not one that could have been considered dangerous. 'Which just shows how wrong one can be, when the sea is involved,' she added.

At the inquest the coroner deplored the lack of lifejackets, but they kept thinking of the red flare they never handed over before they cast off the tow-line. One red flare off Margate, and they would have got to them before the lifeboat. The day they went to the inquest at Broadstairs was one of those still October days, the sun shining steadily out of a cloudless sky.

'Between the two Forelands, and north across the downs to the 20 mile expanse of water that was the Thames Estuary, the sea was as smooth as silk, the little waves rolling up the beaches to the chalk cliffs with scarcely a murmur, horizon and sky merging in a faint haze. All the trippers had gone. The lightest of south-easterlies stirred the first yellow leaves across the pavement and our reason for being there did not seem to make sense. Impossible, looking at the faint lip of the Margate sand shining in the serene sunlight, to believe that it had seen and knew all the secrets of what we were trying to piece together for the magistrate.

'The result would only be guesswork. And in the sun the warm waves broke and the seagulls rose up to follow a small fishing-boat plodding towards Longnose,' Kath recalled.

Later Mike – who had sailed on *Snipe* – had his own theory about what had caused her to founder. Her shroud lashings had been of natural cord, reeved through the eyes of the galvanised wires and through the chain-plates several times. Mike thinks that once they got wet they shrank and pulled the keel-stepped mast downwards with such pressure it pushed her keel loose which split the boat apart.

The East Coast Area Old Gaffers Association still award the Tom Bolton cup in their annual race – he had once entered *Maria* into an OGA race with John and Jack as crew.

Mike came close to shipwreck himself one night on a passage from Heybridge Basin on the Blackwater back round to Fambridge on the Crouch. For crew he had the larger than life character Jimmy Green, famous for hoisting his beer gut onto the counter at the Ferry Boat, and ordering the barmaid to 'fill it up please' and oil company rep Tony Robinson. It was Tony's first ever sail. The night was pitch black apart from the falling snow and the wind strong from the north. In such blizzard conditions they were sailing down through the Rays'n Channel between the Dengie Flat which had been used as a bombing range during the war. Four barge hulks were used to mark the target area and they were covered at high water. Fortunately Tony was standing with his head poking through the fore-hatch when he saw one of the snow covered hulks in the murk dead ahead. His shouted warning enabled Mike to put the helm over just in time. 'Even if we'd only started a plank we would have been goners,' Mike recalled.

Tony told me later at his tidy brick home on a new estate behind Burnham: 'Mike didn't really lay up as other yachtsmen did. He was a die-hard. On one occasion, having come off the dry dock in Clements Green Creek, we had to row ahead of his boat breaking the ice with an oar. He was the unofficial commodore of what we called the Flexible Yacht Club, not that he would ever expect to be called that, he was too modest.' Members of the FYC would arrange a passage to, say, Pin Mill but if the wind was north-east by the time they got to the Whitaker they would sail instead to Queenborough or vice versa. Whatever destination gave them a fair wind decided the passage.

Tony did not have his own boat but was one of a crew pool who turned up with sleeping bag and oilskins when required, as the Flexible Yacht Club philosophy

dictated. They were known as 'equipage'. They were in the same area when disaster struck a Burnham boat on a night passage in heavy weather returning from an Easter cruise to Ostend. The crewman in question had come on watch on a 28 ft hard chine plywood yacht called *Ally Sloper*, which had left the Belgian port the same time as *Sugar Creek*, and been swept overboard from the bridgedeck by a breaking wave.

Ostend was where a new FYC member received his spurs. Having crossed the North Sea he was entitled to fly the FYC burgee: a Heineken beer flag, obtainable from most garages.

Although Clements Green Creek was still used for its drydock, *Lillian*, and the scrubbing grid, *Sugar Creek*'s draught had necessitated joining the mooring trots at Fambridge where the Fambridge Yacht Club HQ was a wooden shack perched on the sea wall. It had once been a prefabricated hospital in the Crimean War.

'This is where we became "proper yachtsmen",' Mike told me, 'there were yachtsmen here who fitted white covers to their peaked caps when British Summer Time started.' It was as exclusive in its own way 'as the Royal Yacht Squadron: you couldn't get a mooring there unless you had a boat that the trotman, Mr Meiklejohn approved of,' he added. *Sugar Creek* was an approved vessel and as Mr Mick, as the moorings proprietor was known, got to know Mike and realised he worked freelance, he offered him delivery jobs. As it was nearly always a Friday night that the deliveries started, Mike would shine his torch over the delivery's pump handle. 'If it was shiny we knew we would have to watch her in heavy weather'. On one trip, fate played its mysterious hand. The delivery was from Fambridge to the Solent and crewing for Mike was another freelance artist, John Smith, who lived locally. As they motored past Burnham, the throttle lever sheared off and they stopped and left the

PEYTON

boat with a yard to get it replaced. When they recommenced the trip, John told Mike the broken lever was his 'lucky charm' as he'd been offered two months' work in Canada while he'd been at home. As soon as the delivery was over John went off on his new commission but was drowned during a white-water rafting trip.

Mike himself narrowly avoided disaster when the keel dropped off *Tarika*, a newly built 33 ft Kings Amethyst, two days after he and four equipages brought her back to Fambridge from the Polish port of Gdansk on the Baltic.

• 14 •

Chris Doyle comes to Essex

Mike had sailed *Sugar Creek* in the first Old Gaffers Race in 1962 coming fifth at 0130! The race organisers had asked if he would take a professional photographer with him to record the race. This introduced Mike to cameras and he bought a Yashikamat for £40 and went on to produce several covers for yachting magazines including *Yachting Monthly* and *Yachting World*. He also sold his first yachting cartoon to a now defunct fortnightly paper, *Yachting and Boating*, whose editor Charlie Jones became a good sailing friend. Charlie would later lose his job for writing a scathing editorial about the commercial pressures visited upon the Corinthian sport of sailing by the introduction of big prize money. In 1968 *The Sunday Times* had launched their Golden Globe solo, non-stop, round-the-world race in which Donald Crowhurst, a father of four, had remortgaged his home, and apparently committed suicide after fraudulently making up his voyage when he realised the boat was not seaworthy enough to complete the circumnavigation and that he would be financially ruined if he turned round and sailed home.

Mike was also asked to go and see Bernard Hayman, editor of *Yachting World*, who pointed out that he had sited a winch incorrectly in one of his cartoons. 'This made me realise I could not work for such a pedant...especially as *Sugar Creek* didn't have any winches.' It would be Hayman's loss as he later realised, telling Mike he wished he'd given him a staff job.

Mike's sailing was now giving him a living. The demand for his cartoons was slowly but surely picking up, and his delivery work was allowing him access to more boats and more sailors which all provided material for his pencil. Sailing was also providing Kath with inspiration, too. One of the FYC members was an ex-barge skipper, Reg Watson, who had also been the last ferryman at Fambridge. He lived in a house on the marsh. He told stories of barging during World war 1, loading freights of coke from Calais for the Beckton gas works, the maroon piles of which stand like China's Terracotta Army in Gallions Reach on the Thames to this day. He mentioned an anchorage he used called Abraham's Bosom: a giant bight in the Maplin Sand near the Blacktail Spit. Mike was fascinated and wanted to try it out and Kath decided she would write a novel about the Calais run. A cruise to both produced *Thunder in the Sky*, her 11th book.

A three week cruise to the West Country which ended in Salcombe had re-built Kath's confidence at sea. It had helped that they pottered around in Poole Harbour, Studland and Dartmouth en route with beaches and long walks for the children. So when the time came to make the long passage home Kath opted for *Sugar Creek* rather than British Rail. Mike had a strong crew: John Young, a fisherman, and Fred Macey, a foreman at Tilbury Docks and an ex-Merchant Navy seaman, so Kath could concentrate on looking after the girls.

They left Salcombe on a perfect morning, with the sky 'milky and sunshot, the dun falls of the Devon cliffs hazy to port, and the sea mild and pearly to infinity in all other directions'. The wind was light but fair, from the north, but died away to nothing some 10 miles out from Start Point and the haze came down, bright with sunshine but impenetrable. Kath was on the foredeck with the two girls, away from the noise of the engine, and 'we watched the old boat dipping and rolling into the glassy swell, laying back the marblings of foam over the darkness of the water beneath'. Kath composed her mind for a long passage, shutting out the unpleasant possibilities. Thick fog in a shipping lane was unnerving, and they were on the steamer track bound round Portland Bill, as the intermittent lowing of fog-horns proved. 'We stared uneasily into the damp bright wool of our surroundings...we were on edge; the water was perfectly tame and harmless, but the uneasiness would not go away, the boat blind, the fog-horns eerie and queasy in the damp air.'

In the evening Kath put the children to bed, weary of keeping them amused all day, and then turned in herself. She was later woken by the chuckle of a bow-wave and was uplifted at the thought that *Sugar Creek* was sailing again. But she was at anchor in 30 fathoms some 10 miles south of Portland Bill. Mike and crew had bent on all spare warps, and it was just the sound of the foul tide running past.

With a white flare at the ready they waited for the tide to turn 'but the unnaturalness of being anchored in the middle of the sea put me back in hate mode again, forgetting the lovely holiday, aware only of the mean tricks the sea resorted to'. By dawn *Sugar Creek* was motoring again through a dead-calm, but gradually the fog grew thinner. They saw a small coaster on a strange course astern of us, which Mike assumed was going to take him into Weymouth.

'Never having had any reason to distrust Mike's navigation which, although done with a comb or a knife more often than with a ruler or a pair of dividers, is remarkably accurate. I was not surprised when our first sight of land – Anvil Head – proved him right. Later, when Mike at the tiller asked for the position, a member of the crew solemnly told him he was one and a half teaspoons south south west of the Nab.' The fuel was getting very low, and there was still not a breath of wind, the sky was now cloudless with gulls drifting up like gliders in the rising thermals. *Sugar Creek* plugged on as the children started to hit each other, and they could see Swanage Bay beyond the white water slopping over Peverill Bar. But would *Sugar Creek* save her tide into the anchorage? Fish and chips and ice-cream was promised the children as, slowly, slowly, hot and dogged, *Sugar Creek* crept round the buoy and opened up the bay. Under the glassy water they saw the sand and the anchor went down. They had made it but it had been a struggle.

'Performance,' Mike said. 'What we want is performance.'

'Or a great big engine,' said Kath.

Sugar's fate was sealed, Mike was tired of the heavy old boat, not to mention all the maintenance she required. She'd been expensive too; shipwrights had built a new cockpit and bulwarks.

Gaffers were not easy to sell then, but a young student from London University had the romantic idea of setting off on a round-the-world cruise and Colin Archers had become the benchmark for ocean sailing. But Chris Doyle, who sailed from Itchenor, did not expect to find one in Essex, a county he'd never been to before. 'I came out of

"YOU CAN'T BEAT IT; A GOOD SAIL, A QUIET DRINK THEN BACK TO A
SNUG LITTLE CABIN"

the railway station and got into Mike's car. "I am afraid the brakes aren't working" he said, "but it's not a problem, it's very flat around here."' Chris wondered whether this was some kind of Essex humour, after all, Mike was a cartoonist, but soon realised he wasn't joking as he drove 'very sedately and did not once touch the brake pedal'.

'When we arrived at his house he eased the car into the garage where he bought it to a stop against a large bit of wood he had placed there for just that purpose.'

They took *Sugar Creek* out for a trial sail on the Crouch.

'It is now hard to imagine, but in those days she was big and imposing compared to most of the small cruisers people sailed. This was an age when a Nicholson 36 was regarded with the kind of awe we reserve today for a superyacht,' Chris told me. '*Sugar Creek* sailed easily in the river, her big gaff sails filling out magnificently. Down below I fell in love with the massive timbers that held her together and the cosy coal stove. I was sold. The boat reeked of romance from the bowsprit to the massive single cylinder petrol-paraffin engine, which, when you could persuade it to start, sounded a wonderful tonk, tonk, tonk noise.'

Chris bought *Sugar Creek*, and 'in some kind of unwritten contract she came complete with a shipwright and boatyard at South Woodham Ferrers'. This was Peter Pointer who 'lived in a tidal creek at the end of nowhere'. Chris's memory of the Peytons' world is vivid:

'Even to arrive by train was an event, the station had no electricity; you stepped onto the dimly lit platform to the sound of a dozen Tilley lamps. A longish walk

Chris Doyle in the Caribbean

down a completely black country lane ended at a sea wall and Peter's boat yard, which was, incidentally, registered as a farm in order to save Peter from various legal complications. Peter had many animals, but the only dozen you might reasonably associate with a farm were eleven chickens and a donkey. When one of the chickens keeled over from old age, it was not eaten, but received a burial with full honours in respect of its ten years or so of devoted companionship. Realising that this small menagerie might not satisfy the agricultural department's definition of a farm, Peter would also report some two thousand ducks, which was the number of wild ducks he estimated landed on his property on a busy day. But his real love of animals was for the exotic. Upon entry into the workshed I quickly learned to duck low because the curtain rod over the door was the favourite upside down roost of Fred the fruit bat, whose biggest pleasure in life was to swipe at some unsuspecting person with the big hooks on the tips of his wings. His second pleasure was to heft himself the right way up for a few seconds and pee. But Fred was not the only non-human inhabitant of the room. Sitting on a series of badly sagging electrical wires (apparently farms did not need electrical inspection) was an African hornbill, which was constantly moulting. There were also Peter's three dogs which monopolised the only chairs in the room while the rest of us sat on the floor. One of the dogs had its own pets, or so we were assured by Peter: the guinea pigs. True, Peter fed and housed them, but the dog in question liked to spend all day staring at them. Peter also had other strange animals dotted around the farm including a racoon which was always escaping and eating the neighbour's chickens.'

Chris and a friend, Paul Tobias, spent two years of weekends preparing *Sugar Creek* for her Blue Water cruise, as she lay in one of Peter's mud-berths. The shipwright helped him install a new Lister diesel engine, and step a new mast. Before she was copper sheathed, Peter moved the barge out into the middle of the creek, pulled out a series of plugs and let her sink. *Sugar Creek* was floated into the barge, then as the tide went out, propped up. The plugs were then replaced and on the next high tide the barge floated and moved back alongside the sea wall.

'Peter was wonderful, he did occasionally charge me for a few of the many hours he put in, but I don't think I ever paid a cent for berthing or hauling. He also kept a stock of trenails, the ancient wooden pegs which were probably used to join planks to frames around the time of Noah, and he knew how to put them in.

'I came to really appreciate Essex, and its mud, especially after personally enlarging a mud berth for *Sugar Creek* by hand. It was not long before I was laughing at Mike's cartoon of two figures walking into the mud. One is from Essex

"THAT'S ALRIGHT I DON'T MIND A BIT OF MUD.
WE HAVE IT ON THE SOUTH COAST TOO"

with thigh length waders, the other wearing those shorty boots that stop above the ankle. The latter was saying something like: "Well you know, we have mud on the south coast too".

In 1967 Chris, his girlfriend Nikki, who would become his first wife, and Paul Tobias sailed *Sugar Creek* successfully to the Mediterranean where they spent six months before crossing the Atlantic to the Caribbean where they, too, chartered the boat for day cruises until they had enough money to buy some land in Grenada. Paul jumped ship in Cayenne, French Guiana, and became a shrimp trawler skipper. He later returned to the UK and Clements Green Creek to ask Peter Pointer to help find him his own yacht. 'I was very sad not to find him there. I was also sad to see that a housing estate had grown up on the road leading down to his place,' Paul told me. He eventually found a yacht and sailed her back to the West Indies.

Chris and Nikki lived aboard the boat while they built a house on Grenada. When Chris decided he wanted to bare boat charter he sold *Sugar Creek* and bought *Rustler of Arne*, a 32 ft Rustler. *Sugar* took her new owner off round the Caribbean until she was sold again to a native of Bequia. She eventually broke up at anchor in a big hurricane-induced swell. Chris sails the Caribbean to this day continually updating his successful series of pilot books.

'I returned once, many years later, to Essex to look at where my dream of sailing away to islands with beaches and palm trees began. There was nothing left, just row after row of new houses; it was as if the whole place and time was something I just dreamed up.' In the late 1970s the 'plotland' of South Woodham Ferrers with its ramshackle houses, including Long Acre, was sold to speculators who bulldozed it all away to build the new town which buried Chris's memories and which stands there today with street names like Spinnaker Way and Starboard View, the only reminders

Chris, Paul and Nikki prepare *Sugar Creek* in Clements Green Creek, for the Caribbean

of the ghosts it laid to rest. Kath remembers the arrival of one land speculator who tried to ingratiate himself with her family by giving the girls half a crown. 'It infuriated her,' said Mike, 'as he had just incurred major inflation with their pocket money.'

Clements Green and Fenn Creeks still wind their muddy fingers around each flank of closely packed brick homes, but now they are feared as agents of rising sea level which could spoil expensive real estate rather than a phenomenon to be lived with. The modern world has too many trappings to be balanced on a table during big tides. Apart from a few dinghies at Eyott Sailing Club, hauled up on the grass at Fenn Creek, and the rotting hulk of *Lillian*, Peter Pointer's barge at the head of the dammed Clements Green Creek, all the boats and the moorings in the creeks have gone.

Mike wanted to sail a boat which was a lot handier than the heavy old Colin Archer. Plywood had revolutionised yacht building and other FYC members had built their own boats. Ian Griffiths, a local headmaster, had made *Thyatira*, a 25 ft *Yachting World* Junior Offshore Group Lightcrest, a Frers design, and sailed her to Norway and back. But when Mike came aboard he wasn't impressed with the accommodation: 'It's like living under the kitchen table,' was his undiplomatic remark. Another local, Mick 'the brick' Wilkins, a bricklayer, had built his own *Eventide* which had more room down below, but Maurice Griffiths, her designer, was never famous for producing a pretty boat. Mike had raced aboard Stellas at Burnham-on-Crouch and loved their performance and sweet lines and toyed with the idea of buying one, but as he had once been pooped in *Sugar Creek* he decided he wanted a boat with a bridgedeck and self-draining cockpit which the Stella does not have.

Froyna proved to be the nearest Folkboat for sale, at the right price. She was the conventional clinker-built Norwegian variety, without a dog-house. Her owner had bought one of the new, 'flashier' (as Mike saw it) Polish types, with a big dog-house, but he preferred the thoroughbred type, in spite of her spartan accommodation. And after *Sugar Creek* she was spartan, with barely sitting headroom in the saloon, and no coal stove. Having been used as a dayboat, she did not even have a galley. But she was a 'yacht', Mike's performance vessel with a 10 hp Albin, which drove her at such a rate of knots 'she put her stern down like a speed-boat'. The engine worried Mike at first, it was an embarrassment with its excess of power, 'but like all luxuries, one gets used to them very quickly'. It was the first week in March when Mike sailed her home from Walton-on-Naze, and it snowed hard all the way, 'Although he didn't admit it, I know he missed *Sugar*'s glowing stove,' said Kath. Only once he'd sold her did Mike confess: 'It was like sleeping in a snowball.'

With his new sailing machine Mike became very competitive. 'Sailing was now no more than a deadly duty to beat the others. In *Sugar*, it was either her conditions – when she was unbeatable – or it wasn't, when one just didn't worry. But in *Froyna* we were now evenly matched with a good many of our neighbours, and sailed in company with three or four other boats every weekend and whoever was on the tiller was expected to keep *Froyna* in front. Or at least have a good excuse for not doing so. I always had plenty of excuses.'

Hilary, was showing signs of ousting her mother as first mate, but Veronica merely retired to the nearest bunk and waited to arrive.

As far as work was concerned, Kath painted little *Froyna* in a twinkling, although with a good deal of blasphemy when it came to cutting in the boot-topping on the clinkerous turn of the bilge. Mike installed a galley, and *Froyna* was 'finished'. Although Mike loathed maintenance and DIY – both got in the way of actually sailing – he felt strangely lost without a job to be done. As a result he was lured round to Fenn Creek which 'housed a variety of wrecks', where he had heard about a project. He was inspired by the Frank Shuttlewood-built five-ton cutter, which Fred Macey had restored at Fenn Creek from wreck to going concern.

The remains of *Lillian*, dry dock to Mike and many others, in Clements Green Creek

With Fred's bargain in their minds, they contemplated a derelict Leigh bawley, *Amy*, that lay on her side, the ebbing tide draining out of her seams.

They joked that it was only the horseshoe nailed to her transom that had seen her make a passage to Calais and back, not long before. She had been sailed there by her owner, Jimmy Green, who had literally sawn her mast off, to enter the French canals. For the return trip he had 'reassembled' it with some metal straps screwed to both parts. Jimmy was now looking for a 'proper yacht' and sold her, 'with the dinghy', to Mike for £15. She was caulked with Essex clay, had a tarpaulin for a mainsail and a 'Trespassers will be prosecuted' signboard for a rudder. *Froyna* towed *Amy* round to Clements Green Creek where she was dry docked in *Lillian*. In theory the process was quite straightforward, but in fact *Lillian* hardly ever sank at the first try, which generally meant the next tide in the middle of the night, when everyone had to muster again. This happened on one occasion when they were all going to a New Year's Eve party in fancy dress, so that at one o'clock in the morning a very strange assortment of people was to be seen roaring out in the darkness, including a St Trinian's schoolgirl and a station-master in a bowler hat.

On this occasion the barge disappeared, with a 'quiet sigh and mere bubbles of surrender to mark her passing'. Once dried out in the barge, *Amy* looked, to her joint owners' eyes, full of potential. No one else saw her in that light including Peter Pointer who was going to have to do the serious work. Fred, patting her hull, said, 'This boat doesn't need new chain-plates, but I reckon these chain-plates need a new boat'. Some 28 ft long, and with a beam of 11 ft, *Amy* was one of the original Leigh bawleys, a corruption of 'boiler boats', built for shrimping on the shoals of the Thames Estuary. They used to come complete with a boiler for cooking the shrimps in, so that the catch was ready to sell as soon as they got it home.

Fenn Creek today, with modern South Woodham Ferrers encroaching

Looking back on it now it seemed a daft and rather pointless idea, trying to get *Amy* rebuilt but Mike was still very attracted by traditional boats and felt he was backsliding, having exchanged a noble classic for a frippery yacht. He felt great sympathy towards *Amy* and her kind, left to rot in narrow creeks and, in so doing, taking into limbo a whole way of life, insufficiently recorded and only too soon to be forgotten.

They had plans to remove her 'horrible dog-house' and knock out her rotten decks, but 'although we were willing labour-wise, we aren't much good with tools when it comes to practical things'. As reality set in *Amy* finished as a 'magnificent bonfire' on the shores of the creek, 'but provided many hours of the most pleasant way of wasting time, and is remembered with affection,' Kath said.

Both shared a habit for using old ship's parts as object d'art. Rookery Cottage has the taffrail of the old Ramsgate sailing trawler *Problem* in the front room bolted to the wall as a mantelpiece. *Problem*, built in 1904, fished for most of her life out of Lowestoft, before ending her days hulked in Lion Creek. Her mast was still standing in the 1960s. In another room hangs the steering wheel of the sailing barge *Nell Gwyn*, also hulked at nearby Althorne Creek. She was built in 1907, became a barge-yacht after she went out of trade, then a houseboat, before finally falling apart. The living room has a curtain across the door that is held up with big brass rings looped over a lighter sweep, which Mike found drifting in the Thames. His study is wallpapered with charts of the Thames Estuary and a lounge table is made from 2 ins thick barge boards. In the garden the well-painted original rudder of his current boat *Touchstone* serves as a patio table. One feature of its design is a step in the trailing edge. This was used as a 'ladder' to help anyone who fell overboard and was used in anger twice.

• 15 •

A Brush with the RNLI

On a day of bright sunshine and a strong south-west wind, two boats bashed into the green waves beneath Cap Griz Nez as they beat to Boulogne. Any Frenchman interested enough to train his binoculars on the dancing white sails beneath him would have been puzzled to note that both yachts were flying Heineken beer flags. *Froyna* and *Thyatira* were sailing in company and for once were being inflexible: going determinedly upwind not down. The Peyton family plus Fred Macey were on their new boat, and headmaster Ian Griffiths and professional character Jimmy Green were on the boat which inspired the purchase. *Froyna* was shouldering deluges of water over her decks but she was making impressive headway compared to the sluggardly old *Sugar*, taking the more direct path through instead of over the water. 'Our oilskins were streaming and I was very sick, although not too far gone not to enjoy the sight of enormous cloud shadows chasing their way over the tawny empty downs of the Pas de Calais and swooping to darken the glittering water,' Kath noted.

Once in Boulogne, naturally, such a good sail had to be celebrated, but not by Kath who was more concerned about getting Hilary and Veronica to sleep. In this she was successful, but lay awake herself as the menfolk were taking an inordinately long time to return. She lay in her bunk in the summer heat, Boulogne's tart, fishy smell hemmed in by the high harbour walls. Eventually she dozed off, but was woken up at 2am the following day by the recital of 'that awful dirge' she'd heard so many times before. Barge skipper Bob Roberts, still sailing *Cambria* with cargo – the last to do so – had made 'The Bargeman's Alphabet' a popular tune with many yachtsmen, especially those who shared his world from Great Yarmouth to Southampton. Yachtsmen related to Bob – although he made a point of not relating to them – because in those days they, like him, either sailed without engines, or engines that were underpowered, real auxiliaries. Consequently, like *Cambria*, they worked the tides and often anchored off.

Kath lay in her bunk waiting for the awful dirge to finish. But Ian, who was singing it to the accompaniment of his squeeze box and Jimmy beating time on a biscuit tin and Mike and Fred

Kath at helm of *Froyna* with Jimmy Green

Froyna, Mike's 'performance' yacht

joining in the chorus, could not get beyond Q. Instead of moving onto R, Ian went back to A hoping that by the time he got to Q he would remember what Q signified on a Thames barge. Then Kath came up on deck.

'Ian was hanging by his legs upside down from the boom playing his squeeze box. Veronica looked at me from her bunk and said with eight-year-old gravity, "They are drunk, aren't they?" Stone-cold sober myself, I agreed frigidly, but after Ian fell headfirst down the hatch things became a little quieter,' she recalled.

Ian told me at his Rochford home, still a little chastened 40 years later: 'Kath knew what Q was for, but she jolly well wasn't going to say!'. No cartoon was ever drawn about the event and before dawn *Thyatira* had departed, leaving Mike and Fred to face a different kind of music, alone.

Froyna was too small for Mike's purposes

Froyna sailed round to Calais prior to hopping back across the Channel and her crew visited the harbourside church and lit a candle for a safe passage, Mike explaining to the girls the religious significance of the tradition. 'The children liked the idea very much and wanted to light a big fat one but Mike said hastily that a little one would be just as good and half the price, I could see him thinking.' When they left Calais harbour, it blew a Force 7 dead on the nose and, 5 miles out, put about and sailed back in. Kath and the children caught the next ferry back to Dover, later Mike and Fred made a record passage – 13 hours – back to Fambridge, but as Kath said: 'the children were never much impressed by the candle ritual since'.

The following summer the family sailed *Froyna* direct to Cherbourg with the intention of cruising to Brittany, 'but, as usual, we went somewhere else.' They did get a bit further west to Omonville, 8 miles away, set in a wild and romantic-looking coastline with only three tiny cottages in sight. Kath had long imagined the place from a photograph taken by Adlard Coles for his pilot book. She was not disappointed with the reality. 'These are the harbours I love, not the town harbours. Of course these are the harbours fraught with dangers, where one has to turn and run if the weather blows up or blows onshore, but Omonville was kind and perfect, and we lay there for three days,' said Kath. Old grey houses and farms, running inland, were all grown over with pink roses, and the water meadows and hillsides all thick with flowers. They climbed up the cliff top by the ruins of the old fort from where Adlard Coles had taken his bewitching photograph, and lay on the turf in the hot sun. There was a spring lower down, and the farmer's milking buckets lying beside it, shining clean, and the water coming icy through hanging ferns and dark moss asprawl with stonecrop and honeysuckle. The girls were darting about like lizards, in their element, and Mike and Fred lay with the binoculars, watching a small red yacht sailing into the harbour, working out what tide he must have caught and where he had come from to arrive there now, where he should anchor, when to start taking in sail. In Omonville there is scarcely room for three yachts to anchor; he brought up in exactly the right spot.

'Full marks,' Mike said.

Next *Froyna* set sail for Alderney, and made a cautious entry into Braye harbour. From the sea, Alderney looked rather bleak and heavily fortified. Kath treated herself to a hotel room for a night, which had a bathroom overlooking a 'perfect' beach. She bathed in fresh, warm water as she watched the children bathe in cold seawater.

They stayed over a week, the children playing on the beach, Mike and Fred exploring the Nazi forts and museum of occupation. 'There was a very convenient heat haze day after day which was a good nautical excuse for not moving. "All those rocks," we said happily, looking at them disappearing into the haze from the top of the cliffs, "dangerous". We couldn't see the notorious Casquets at all, nor France nor Guernsey, only the nearer rocks with their tide-white teeth gleaming in the sunshine.'

One evening they lay on the cliffs watching a yacht coming up the Swinge, hustling along in the beginnings of the dusk, the tide almost ready to turn. 'She was large, about 50 feet, an old sloop, and an impressive sight from where we watched, hurrying through the troubled waters of the channel in the last misting gleams of light, the whole dusky backdrop of the ocean beyond,' said Kath. Mike and Fred reckoned she was alright; she would make it before the tide turned, and they had a

Drying clothes on *Froyna* after a dowsing at sea

drink in the pub before following a cow track back to the harbour. Here they were amazed to see the old sloop *Piet Hein* sailing into the tiny, drying, Crabby Harbour where *Froyna* lay against the wall. As she entered between the two walls, she grounded, not surprisingly as she drew some 9 feet and the tide was ebbing fast – so fast that she was obviously not going to be refloated until the next tide. And if she lay over, she was going to lay right on one of the harbour walls.

As they watched spellbound, a woman's head popped up out of the afterhatch and called out to all the crew on deck, 'Dinner's ready'.

With Mike's and Fred's assistance warps went out in all directions to hold the boat upright. The skipper called it 'putting up the big top' and had obviously done it before. He completed the whole operation with a spirit level laid on deck!

She was carrying a six-strong charter party: 'We were a bit late on our tide,' her skipper said, 'because we went in to have a look at the gannets. Come and have a drink.'

At dawn when the tide rose, the spider's web of warp around the yacht was retrieved and the yacht was berthed against the wall, but – her lines untended – she moved 6 feet out from the wall, and with the tide ebbing fast once more, she was just beginning to lean inwards in such a way that her mast would shortly be taking the whole weight of the boat.

'Oh, my God,' groaned the skipper after Mike woke him up. But with 'the same cheerful ingenuity he had displayed the night before', he pumped up two rubber dinghies and laid them over as fenders, lashed some oars to his shrouds, wedging the other ends on the crevices in the wall. Then he went back to bed. Later in the day, to show his gratitude, he dropped a bag of cream pastries down to the girls in *Froyna's* cockpit. As it was a drop of about 15 feet and they all fell out of the bag as they descended we then had a very jammy, messy cockpit.

'Oh my God,' he said, 'Come and have a drink'.

On board again, Mike looked at all the beefy crew available to this skipper and thought how they were paying for the privilege. It was something that would not stop gnawing at him: paying hands as opposed to paid hands.

The weather was still very hot and hazy when *Froyna* left Braye bound for Salcombe and the wind was very light. Before they were scarcely clear of the breakwater it died completely. Mike started the engine, but it had only run for a short time when a lug in the drive sheared off completely. They were now helplessly adrift in a four knot tide with the Casquets to port and the rocky landfall of the Cap de la Hague to starboard. Mike decided to anchor, but even with every warp, sheets, even the halyards bent on, could not touch bottom. Visibility was very bad and they could see none of the dangers they knew surrounded them. 'So we sat in the cockpit beneath the slatting boom and hoped we were far enough offshore for all this not to matter.' As darkness fell the visibility improved, and they saw the loom of firstly Cap de la Hague then hours later the Casquets as they drifted on the tide. The sail was barely filled, caving and filling like an ailing lung. There was nothing in sight, but visibility was still poor as it had been all the week. They decided they were out of danger, which was nice, but a little more wind would have been nicer still. All the next day *Froyna* 'crawled over the ocean, leaving behind her mere bubbles to show that we were moving', the forecast promised nothing but ones and twos. Mike had decided to make for Weymouth to shorten the passage, but with the log scarcely registering it was hard to estimate where they were, and all they could do was wait for the darkness to possibly show them some identifiable lights. Portland Bill loomed eventually and at 3am the following day Mike used the dinghy to tow *Froyna* into Weymouth. 'It was the most unexhilarating passage I could remember.'

The RNLI engineer repaired the Albin, telling Mike: 'Small diesels and big filters have knocked the arsehole out of the lifeboat business.' Mike said: 'I've carried big filters ever since.' While the engine was repaired, Fred's brother – who had come to pick him up, his holiday over – drove the crew out to Portland Bill. 'We stood and looked down on the notorious race, looking merely pimply against the rest of the sea, and marked the narrow channel of calm water hard against the rocks that we should be taking the following morning on our way to Devon. The race stretches offshore about five miles, and yachts usually take the inshore route to save the long detour. I have never seen the Portland Race in bad weather, but imagine it must be an awe-inspiring sight.'

The following day the Peytons set out round the Bill, but the wind had gone into the west and was blowing too hard for comfort, so they retreated and set out again a day later when it had moderated. They could not lay their intended destination, Torbay, and instead by evening nosed into Exmouth, 'which proved a tortuous, unkind place for a foreigner, with a fierce tide and lot of sand in places where the chart said there was a channel'. The wind blew up hard and the following day they went up to Powderham, but went aground in the channel. Although it was a rising tide it took more than an hour to get off, as the orange sand boiled up round the hull in a most inhospitable way. They decided it was a port for 'local knowledge', which they were fast acquiring by hard experience. When they left the following day, Mike decided local knowledge included following a fishing-boat back out to sea and went hard aground on the sand-bar opposite the beach. This time it was on the ebb and they knew immediately that they were there for the day, 'a nice target for the sixpenny telescope mounted on its pedestal on the promenade across the fast-flowing channel'. At least, Kath thought, they had this particular beach to themselves, but Mike was not very happy about the way in which *Froyna* dried out. The sand had built up on one side of the hull so that it was up to the deck, and on this bank she lay only 10 degrees off being upright, but on the other side there was a scoured hole right down to the keel and a pool full of shrimps and baby crabs; 'It was very undignified, right opposite the beach, and there was no excuse for it, but the children thought it was a good place.' In the afternoon a boat came past and the men in it said they manned the local inshore lifeboat, and would keep an eye on them when they lifted. We thanked them, touched by their solicitude, but things did not work out as amiably as they expected.

There was quite a fresh breeze, and when the water came back they were surprised by the fury with which it roared up over the sand. All the same Mike had laid out the anchor where he wanted it and, although they knew it was going to be uncomfortable for a time, they were not worried, especially as *Froyna* was propped up on her own sandbank at a reasonable angle. The children came back on board and they got everything stowed, and the water came pouring into the shrimp pool, slapping over the keel, very agitated, white-crested all over the shoal. They sat on the deck, feeling *Froyna*'s uneasy stirrings beneath them. Then they heard the roar of engines and the inshore rubber lifeboat came racing out from the beach. One of the men got out and waded over.

'We'll take a line and pull you off,' he said.

Mike was a bit doubtful, and explained where he had laid out the anchor, and mentioned the bank *Froyna* had made for herself. They would rather have got off themselves, but submitted to the local knowledge of the RNLI. The lifeboatman waded out to get the anchor. It was hard work in the racing tide, but he brought it back and Mike gave him a line which he took back to the inflatable with him.

'It's too soon yet surely?' Kath said. But the locals thought otherwise.

'Bloody hell,' Mike muttered as the powerful outboard opened up. As *Froyna* started to bump and strain he said a lot more things, and went up on the foredeck and yelled and waved his arms, and the lifeboatmen yelled back. Mike wanted them to pull the other way, but they were trying to pull *Froyna* over her sandbank. They wouldn't go the other way. And *Froyna* wouldn't go their way, although they were trying hard enough. Mike was raging, and across the white, swirling sandbank a fierce altercation took place. Nobody could properly hear what the other side was saying, but old local knowledge met new local knowledge in a summit of, er, entrenched disagreement.

'My gentle mental lifelong vision of the lifeboatman as a cross between Jesus and a nautical Father Christmas took a hard knock,' said Kath, 'It occurred to me that no doubt in the heat of most rescues a lot of invective must invariably take place but this, over what was not after all a matter of life and death, did seem very sad at the time and I went below and brooded.'

When *Froyna* was off – with her keel still intact – Mike and the lifeboatmen parted on perfectly amiable terms. 'Did you pay them?' asked Kath. 'Yes,' said Mike

with a sigh. 'That'll teach you to follow fishing-boats,' said Kath, never a spouse to leave her mind unspoken. The next day they sailed on to Salcombe and sailed through a spectacular storm off Teignmouth, with a rainbow standing across the cliffs and the sea stark yellow with hidden sunlight, the sky crashing overhead. They hove-to and made tea. Later *Froyna* entered Salcombe just in time, before the wind backed from south-west to south – the worst direction for that Devonshire idyll – and spent a wild night dragging in a southerly gale, until they found an unoccupied buoy. Then, in the morning, they were given a mooring in the Bay, and lay there happily for several days with nothing harder to cope with than the row to the shops.

They had given the Folkboat a fair crack of the whip, but for long-distance cruising with a family of four she was too small. More importantly Mike tried all ways to fit a coal stove into her for winter sailing but it was impossible. During this, just their second summer with her, Mike took to reading advertisements again, and put her up for sale, hoping she wouldn't go until the end of the season. But one balmy evening the Peytons found a doctor and his wife sitting on board, having arrived in Fambridge from London.

'Shall we have a little sail?' Mike asked, and the four of them crept up the river into the golden eye of the setting sun, and the boat was out of their hands from that moment. For Mike 'it was inevitable, and distinctly annoying, but what he had asked for'.

· 16 ·

Anchor Dragging

Mike took to haunting boatyards and boat-builders and disappeared for whole evenings under mounds of shiny literature. He wanted something about 30 ft, and tried for a long time to work out a way of getting a glass-fibre boat at the sort of price they could afford, but it was impossible. It was 1968 and large wooden boats were comparatively much cheaper, particularly as it was at the time of a fierce credit squeeze, and it was the very large ones that were the most tempting, being very good value for money. They got to the stage of thinking about it all in Monopoly terms, quite divorced from reality, and winter drew in and they looked at the end-of-season bargains, freshly on the market, and the rain dripped steadily through peeling coachroofs and trickled sullenly from the lips of green portholes, and nobody had the boat they wanted.

There was an advert in one of the magazines which concluded: Lying Scunthorpe.

'Scunthorpe?' said Kath who had not registered the town as being one where yachts were owned. But Mike wrote a letter, and received in reply an eight page screed describing the virtues of this 'oddly marooned boat', which included such items as a built-in wireless to port and a built-in record-player to starboard that will play irrespective of heel or movement'. Her inventory included 'Every table and book on navigation celestial and coastal, star charts and plotter, 7 or 8 pilot books and 50 charts from here to Formosa.' The letter finished intriguingly: 'If I can sell her in the next month or so it could save my marriage, hence the cheap price. I hope she is what you are looking for, for she is capable of circling the earth easily and safely.'

He had not anywhere said what this cheap price was, and what with a nautical record-player and a domestic crisis thrown in, they were agog to make tracks for Scunthorpe to see this marvel.

Dowsabel was a yawl, 33 ft LOA 10 ft 5 ins beam, built of larch on oak by Whisstocks of Woodbridge in 1958. 'By our standards she was almost new.' Mike went up to look at her and came back frowning and vague, and sat for hours in his armchair gazing into space. 'He could afford her, but did he want her? seemed to be the big question.'

To help him decide he returned with Kath and four trusted Clements Green Creekers. She lay next to a power station which was belching plumes of dark smoke, and the immediate landscape was as dreary as only a half-industrialised, half wasteland can be. Kath felt it was no place for a Suffolk yacht to lie. It was as if she had succumbed to her surroundings, for she lay grimy and inert, hung with old motor-tyres, her tanned sails rotting on smoke-darkened spars. She had a lifebuoy all in tatters propped against her shrouds; her varnish work was dark with weather. The first impression was not heart lifting.

Dowsabel, a 33 ft yawl was built by Whissocks of Woodbridge

But for Mike she was the right shape and of the right character, and she looked powerful as well as graceful. Mike's faithful friends started making scornful remarks, but the owner put his head out of the hatch and invited them aboard. Mike and Kath went below, as the others started prowling round the deck. One of their number, 'Scotch' Bob White, who had just bought a Vertue, and looked at more boats than any other man on the whole coast of Britain and was considered a hard man to please, got out his penknife. The saloon floor was laid with brown lino and surrounded with bare wood. It was cramped but homely, the wireless was mixing its noise with a whistling kettle. The owner lived aboard, and the whole boat gave the impression of a caravan parked in a canal. The forepeak was so full of junk that one could not get more than a foot inside it. 'The saloon was all carpet slippers and teapots.' We could see Bob was going to have a hard time finding a spot for his penknife.' Curiously the inside of the whole boat had apparently never been painted from new, for all the wood was bare from stem to stern.

'She's only ten years old. And a good builder. There can't be anything much wrong with her.'

'We can get her surveyed anyway.'

'And he's bound to come down in price. Most people wouldn't find her attractive, not like this.'

Mike went into a huddle with the owner and mentioned the survey.

'There's nowhere near here to dry her out,' the owner said.

But Mike had made his own mental survey and 'I knew Mike thought all difficulties were good excuses to get the price down,' said Kath.

The conversation went on for a long time, shoulders hunched against the wind, but at last there was an agreement. They parted and Mike came up, grinning.

Dowsabel ensconced in *Lillian*

'Let's go and find the others.'

'Bursting with achievement and pride we capered into the pub where the others were sitting in a gloomy quartet round an empty fireplace,' Kath recalled.

'Well, what do you think of her?' Mike asked, 'We've bought her.'

There was a long silence.

'What'll you have to drink?' Bob asked tactfully.

'Do you really want to know?' Jimmy Green said.

The most positive light that could be put upon it was that she was heavily built, Bob had found no rot, and the standing rigging looked sound. The sails were rotten, but Mike scrounged around and took a set up with him. Jimmy Green and one other went up to for a December delivery trip. Ian Griffiths helped dock *Dowsabel* safely inside *Lillian*, 'With the dry-dock in place in the middle of the creek we waited for the tide to return so we could dock Mike's new boat. But *Lillian* floated again and we held our breath until enough water gurgled in through the bung holes, then she went down like the *Titanic* with much turbulence.' *Dowsabel*, was given a post-purchase survey and, apart from seven cracked ribs, had a clean bill of health. These were doubled up by Peter Pointer, whose fruit bat by now had been removed to a cage on top of the TV. 'It was a revolting thing, it looked like a moth-eaten umbrella,' Ian told me, 'it was unquestionably male as the only part of it which stuck up the right way was its horribly large penis.'

Kath, who remembered so thankfully bidding farewell to *Sugar Creek* and all her capacious interior which ate up gallons of paint every winter, now had 33 feet of virgin timber to decorate. But first the boat was gutted of its live-aboard clobber. 'Starting with the record-player that played at any angle of heel, we finished off with a load of loose feathers out of the forepeak which must once have constituted a

MARCH 1969 3s 6d

Yachting World

FITTING OUT NUMBER

Kath painting *Dowsabel*, Yachting World cover March 1968

mattress.' Every inch of her was scrubbed down. Then they started on the outside. She was burned off and 'the arduous round of primers and undercoats and topcoats' began. Topcoats were in the grey-blue of which *Sugar Creek* and *Froyna* had been painted. The colour scheme was traditional for East Coast craft although this had nothing to do with its choice. Mike had been given a 45 gallon drum of Admiralty grey which had arrived mysteriously from the Port of London Authority via Tom Bolton. Even the woodwork of Long Acre was battleship grey. It was a good consignment and is still going: as I write this in 2009, his latest boat, *Touchstone*, would do the boat deck of the *Ark Royal* proud.

Aboard *Dowsabel* all the bright-work succumbed too. 'Life is just too short for varnish,' Mike said, as he slapped on the warship gloss.

Mike had reservations about her canoe stern. He had once been pooped in *Sugar Creek* and didn't trust them in a heavy following sea. After Mike's 'carpentry', *Dowsabel* slept six. Almost subconsciously he was thinking of the big sloop in Alderney with the paying crew. 'He used tongue and grooved pine boarding because it was cheap when he made mistakes, which was often,' said Kath. And one day June Griffiths was astonished to watch Mike chewing off unwanted strips of wooden tongue, as he worked, with his teeth. 'It's quicker than sawing or planing,' he explained, looking like a panda with a mouthful of bamboo. The galley consisted of two Primus stoves and a washing up bowl for a sink. Her 10 hp Albin was replaced with an 18 hp version. A coal stove was installed beside the mast close to the skipper's bunk, in the saloon.

The man now making a reasonable living depicting the sailing accidents of others was becoming more cautious and he had hired a life-raft for the trip back from the Humber. He later bought one and carried it in a permanent casing on the cabin top just forward of the mast. *Dowsabel* had a narrow rounded cabin top, having over 6 feet of headroom below, and good roomy sidedecks. She had bulwarks all round about 8 ins high, pulpit, pushpit and good lifelines. Her self-draining cockpit was enclosed by very elegant curving coamings, tapering towards her canoe stern; she had a carved dolphin for a tiller, and was beautifully easy on the helm. The new mainsail, from Jeckylls had two rows of reef-points, which were used often. Their doubts on the canal bank at Scunthorpe were rapidly dispelled by her performance; their sceptical friends ate their words.

The first summer they owned *Dowsabel* they sailed to the Solent with the intention of crossing to Cherbourg and coming back along the French coast to Boulogne. Mike had worked out statistically that in August one should get fair winds all the way after the Solent; 'the only trouble was that when we were in the Solent it blew gales from all directions, fair and otherwise, and we spent a lot of time in Beaulieu and Poole harbour, anchored off the unoccupied end of Brownsea island and getting Lotus-lulled by the undeniable attractions of that lovely spot'. Ian and June Griffiths joined the Peyton family for the cruise.

Anchored in Studland Bay for a day's swimming had been fine with the wind in the west. And they decided to spend the night there. The riding lights sprang up one by one, needling the warm dusk; voices carried over the water, and the soft splash of returning oars and the smell of cooking supper was magic and peaceful. But during the night they woke to the wind in the rigging. Something was wrong. It was all as ominous as it had been comforting a few hours before. The wind had backed round to the east and Studland was now a lee shore, far too close for comfort. The wind came up steadily, with splattering dashes of rain, and in the darkness the riding lights that had shone so kindly now flickered and tossed on plunging forestays. Out on deck they could hear the voices of anxious skippers, a shout now and then as two boats came together. *Dowsabel* kicked and plunged like a lassooed horse, grinding her chain with a noise like the rolling of stones in a mountain torrent.

Mike and Ian kept anchor watch, but as it was pitch dark, they decided to give it an hour until dawn, and then move out, when there should be enough water over Poole bar to get back into the harbour.

At first light, they started to get the anchor in.

'It was a wild and stormy dawn with all the excesses of a Victorian painting, black clouds rolling back over a spray-streaked sea to reveal the wild red flames of a shepherd's warning. *Dowsabel*, lit by the awesome sunrise, flew for the bar under her smallest headsail and mizzen; it was wonderful in the strange dawn, crashing through a glittering sea towards the shore of oblivious, sleeping houses where the alarm clocks had yet to ring, so close to the everyday in fact and yet so far in spirit. It was a typical sailing turnabout, from sweet relaxation to a haring, critical hour when it mattered very much just what one did or didn't do.'

When the smart houses of Poole came to life, and breakfast was being served all along the Bournemouth shore, *Dowsabel*'s crew were going back to their sleeping bags to catch up.

Once the weather settled down they sailed across to Cherbourg with plans to head eastward and explore the Normandy coastline. The next day they sailed into Isigny, a virtually inland town reached by a worrying sail over several miles of drying sands and up a narrow river as far as the town bridge. Here they lay against the wall amongst the mussel-fishing boats, using a borrowed ladder to gain the quay when *Dowsabel* was aground. The cobbled quay petered out past a few cottages on to a sea wall and miles of ditch-seamed pasture, which rolled inland to wooded farmland.

Mike and Ian went out for a day with some mussel fishermen, while June, Kath and the children wandered out into the country along a ditch bright with water lilies and great glistening toads straight out of Grimms fairy tales and, in the churchyard, the grave of Flight Lieutenant Ashpole who had chosen this unlikely spot for his last landfall. There could be worse places to lie, Kath thought, as they wandered through the hot grass. His fate made her more grateful and sensuously aware of the live smell of cows and the trodden white dust, the coolness of the willow shade.

The mussel fishing proved the hardest work that Mike and Ian had experienced for some time and so the girls felt obliged to eat all the mussels that had resulted from such hard labour, and sailed with a large pan on the boil. 'It was still very hot and there was hardly any wind, and we made slow progress, eating mussels for breakfast, lunch and tea.' The mussels lasted the next two days and the womenfolk looked longingly at the finest restaurants of Ouistreham, and Deauville, and Fécamp as yet more damned molluscs were boiled up.

Boulogne left them with only two days in hand to get home so they crossed the Dover Strait through thick fog: Mike had them all on watch, sitting on the cabin top pointing into the wind like setters after duck. They heard a good deal of the unpleasant, anonymous thudding of diesel engines, slow and ominous, and they sounded the foghorn, but saw nothing.

At the Varne buoy, which they picked up with satisfaction, two plovers flew past, very low, and one fell into the water next to the boat. They fished it out with the heads bucket and the children took it below and made it a nest in a locker and fed it, but they were in tears for the other one, all out on its own in the inhospitable fog. An hour later, this peculiar avian Kamikaze act was repeated by another plover and then a pigeon! All three were now in the children's rescue centre.

They learned later that a vast number of racing pigeons were lost that weekend on a flight from France, losing their homing senses in the thick fog.

Eventually they picked up the Folkestone diaphone, and navigated cautiously inshore until the chalk cliffs appeared 'not beyond the bows as usual, but horribly high up in the air, just beyond the spreaders, gleaming with the uncanny sunlight from above'. They anchored in the outer harbour more fortunate than another boat which sailed straight into the cliffs causing some damage. The following day the sun shone and the wind blew and they romped home to Fambridge, releasing the plovers in the mouth of Crouch where they cried and tumbled over the sea wall. The pigeon came home and for several weeks was nursed in a big aviary, but when they eventually let him go he flew up high and homed away south as though nothing had interfered with his French voyage.

'I hope they didn't wring his neck,' Kath thought cheerfully.

There were times when Kath seriously asked herself what she was doing sailing at all. She was regularly seasick and terrified, spent hours under deckheads with a brush, paint dripping on her face, and was tiring of the cursed 'flexibility factor'. As a young mother with two children to organise, the charms to be found with the constant changing of plans was wearing thin. Things came to a head on a bad weather cruise to the West Country. After sailing into Falmouth on a compass course in thick weather they got a rope round the prop. Mike, who lived to be on the water, did not ever want to get in it. He had two daughters and a wife who continually nagged him to find beaches for swimming and so he reasoned it should be one of them who unfouled the prop. 'Now's your big chance,' he said bluntly. After a furious row, Kath had to agree; it was true Mike never had any pretensions of sea-bathing and, in any case, without his spectacles he would be pretty useless.

"IT WAS SIMPLY TOO COLD FOR COMFORT TO DO MORE THAN ONE HOUR
ON WATCH AT A TIME"

Kath pulled on her bathing costume.

'The water was so cold it took all my breath away, and when I put the snorkel and goggles on, the propeller looked about a hundred miles away, very clear and detailed, enmeshed in its blue nylon rope. I put my head up. "How far away is it?" "About three feet," Mike said icily.' But Kath could not reach it and went off for a swim 'to keep up morale'. Mike got his own back by going below, leaving his wife to get back on board via the dinghy. Not speaking, they sailed across to Flushing where a diver cut the rope free.

This silly domestic knocked Kath's confidence and while she was on watch as they sailed back up Channel bound for Fowey she gave way to a boat which was hove-to, but which she thought was on starboard tack. This, not unreasonable error, gave her cause to flagellate herself mentally, 'I am stupid by nature about things nautical. Years of doing it have taught me a certain amount, but it comes hard. I am not a natural. I am not capable of recognising a boat hove-to which, after more than a dozen years, is not very bright.'

They had a leading wind into Fowey and anchored on the Polruan side of the river, but as the southerly wind increased, decided to go on up to Wiseman's Pool, the last deep water anchorage on the river, a mile or two up beyond the china clay jetties, round some good sheltering loops of wooded hillside.

The best places in the pool were taken by moorings, none of which were empty, and they motored round cautiously weighing up the best spot to anchor, aware that the tide was on the ebb and that there wasn't much deep water. On the chart Wiseman's Pool is infallible, sheltered from all directions. In fact, with its banks of oak woods on either side, rising steeply from rocky shores, the valley on this occasion acted like a wind tunnel and, with a very strong tide running against the wind, the anchored boats rode wildly round their scopes, travelling so fast that at times they looked as if they were motoring out. They unbent one of their stowed foresails and dropped it below to reduce windage, but at times the boat lay over almost to the rail. With the wind there was also a horizontal rain, too spiky to face up to but there was no question of staying below. 'The boats were fouling one another; thuds and splintering noises, flashing lights and epithets came out of the darkness. We came up against a large motor-boat, but without damage, then raced across the river towards the eastern shore. The torch showed jagged fingers of rock reaching out, and the limpet roots of the oaks that were tossing with a noise like steam trains.' With the engine in reverse holding them off in the nick of time, the spreaders brought down a 'harvest festival' of oak branches on deck. The motor-boat moved away further up the river. *Dowsabel*'s anchor was relaid five times, and then, hooked up on old cable, held for a while until she started dragging very fast down on to two yachts that had been swooping about each other all night, advancing and retreating like 'dancers in a quadrille, and meeting on occasion with hideous noises'.

While Mike and Hilary furiously hauled in the chain, Kath tried to steer. 'Our anchor was now entangled with loops of rusty iron cable and we were grappling with another boat; torches flashed, Hilary came for a knife. Another boat was looming towards us on the other side. I saw someone rear up to fend off. I didn't know what was going on and put the engine out of gear. It was impossible to hear what anyone shouted in the wind, let alone with the engine noise, but the message came via Hilary that we were clear and to move off, so I went hard in reverse again. Now the wind was so strong that with the 16-horse engine at full throttle she could not answer to the helm, and I could hear the awful rushing noise of the oak trees coming up again. She was heeling under bare poles like a racing dinghy.'

'The tide will turn soon. Then it will be all right,' Mike said. On the flood things settled down and they slept at last. It was 0300.

In the morning the wind had dropped a little, the sun shone and a news broadcast revealed lifeboats were out looking for a yacht full of naval cadets off the Lizard.

They had been stressed but safe in Wiseman's Pool, but for Kath it was a turning point.

· 17 ·

Magna Charter

The reeds were bending to a bitterly cold south-east wind along the banks of the Humber at Winteringham Haven. It blew up the empty streets of this North Lincolnshire village and curled round the corners of the low-roofed farm cottage outside which Mike and I stood stamping our feet until the latch clicked and the burly frame of Melvyn Bray showed us into a low beamed kitchen. 'Come through to the living room. Dad'll be down in a minute. He's just getting dressed.'

We sat in silence with mugs of tea as Melvyn polished a huge brass ship's oil lamp. After fifteen minutes or so the whirring sound of a chair lift slowly, but inexorably, lowered a man into the room. 'Tum, tee, tum,' he muttered, clearly controlling pain. He lifted himself with precise, well-practised movements off the electronic chair and scrabbled for a stick hanging over a radiator and hobbled across the room. 'Dum, dee dum,' he hummed again, his oral tune acting as a teeth-clenched leather strap, before stiffly bending into a big, specially adapted chair. He now used his stick to hook a foot stool across the room and propped an outstretched right leg onto it. 'Put your aid in, dad, so's you can hear them,' said Melvyn.

Now 92, Danny Bray's leg is still full of the shrapnel which knocked him over way back in 1946. He was then in charge of a group of German POWs whose job it was to clear mines around Hamburg so that farmers could get back to work for much needed crop-rearing. Danny knew in what patterns the mines were laid, but a former Wehrmacht sergeant thought he knew better and, ignoring an order from Danny's

Mike and Danny Bray sailed round Britain together

Danny Bray joins a charter party for supper aboard *Touchstone*

Ian and June Griffiths sailed regularly with the Peytons

inferior rank, said he had cleared the fuse of one when in fact he had not. The explosion killed him outright and put Danny in hospital for seven weeks.

As a younger man it had not put him off his sailing on the Humber and he kept a catamaran on the Norfolk Broads for many years, but then he saw an advert in *Yachting Monthly* for coastal chartering. An Essex-based yacht skipper would take five people sailing each weekend, so he decided to take his three sons, David, Stephen and Melvyn, away.

Danny was one of Mike's first charterers and they hit it off straight away. They had both been in the same division during the war and had much else in common. They were both quiet, tough and self-reliant. Once at Hollowshore, Danny and Mike needed to reach the deck when *Touchstone* was dried out. Ian Griffiths was there too and remembered how Danny said: 'Use me as a ladder' and allowed Ian to climb up his stiffened frame. 'They were rough types,' he said.

Tony Robinson recalls sailing aboard *Sugar Creek* with Mike and Kath as they followed the Old Gaffers Race around the Blackwater. 'Suddenly, as we got close to one boat, Mike said "Take the helm, Tony, I'll see you later" and leapt aboard this other boat. He fancied doing a bit of racing. He knew if he'd *asked* me to take her I'd have said no, so there I was expected to sail the boat back to Brightlingsea. Fortunately Kath was more than capable of doing that anyway, but it shows you how laid back he was.' Tony also noticed Mike's Spartan diet. 'He once picked up a piece of stale crust and wrapped it round an old piece of beetroot, making himself an instant sandwich. That was what he was like.'

Mick 'the brick' Wilkins, sitting aboard *Estelle*, his home-built, dandy-rigged 32 ft ferro-cement lugger, at Tollesbury, stoked up his blazing coal stove before telling me that when sailing, Mike would cut the rind off the bacon each morning and put it to one side. On the last day he'd fry up the rind and serve that. 'He told me that's what they used to do when he was a kid.'

Once *Dowsabel* had to anchor off Rye and Tony was sent ashore in the dinghy because they had run out of milk, 'He was a bit forgetful when it came to victualling.'

And another time in *Touchstone* with a party of eight aboard, Mike was anchored at

Mick 'the brick' Wilkins became an expert in
ferro-cement

Tony Robinson learnt to sail with Mike

Burnham in bad weather and a poor
forecast. He had not catered for a full
cruise as he thought they would not be
sailing far. Mike had sailed before with a
fellow cartoonist Keith Waite, whose wife
Renee recalls how she met a group of
Mike's charterers when they were on their
own mooring aboard Keith's Santander
Class yawl, *Rumtub*: 'They were all on that
dreadful *Touchstone* and the food was not
that good. Mike said they'd only be seasick
anyway, and he rowed around cadging
food. He could be a bit mean.' Mike
himself told me that the wreck of a rowing
boat used in a failed attempt at crossing

Renee and Keith Waite – the Fleet Street
cartoonist who sailed with Mike

the Pacific Ocean was brought to Downs Boatyard one year and in it he found the remains
of some freeze-dried food which he took aboard *Touchstone* for the next charter party.
They wolfed it down apparently.

But as I sat talking with Keith Waite, now 82, in his cottage at Pin Mill, the old
cartoonist, smartly dressed in his polished deck shoes and polka dot socks, added:
'He's a fighter and he was very helpful to me when I came back to sailing after a long
absence. He advised me a lot.'

Mike recalls he advertised in *Yachting Monthly* because he would get crew who had
their own oilskins and could steer, *The Spectator* to ensure good company when the
anchor was down, and *The Scout* magazine for enthusiastic learners who would do
anything. He received enough replies to build up, over a year or so, as large a crew list
as he wanted. And he never had to advertise again, as the same people came back for
more every year, bringing their friends. 'The business became quite unbusinesslike in
that the clients turned into friends and the paying part almost an embarrassment –
not so much so that he declined it!' said Kath. One – who came back every year – even

Mike, bikes and *Touchstone*

carved his name on a deck beam over his bunk and demanded the same berth each time. Occasionally Mike would get a corporate job, like the BBC series about celebrities afloat he was hired for. He remembers Alf Garnett, the comic actor, being a 'good bloke' because he sailed anyway, but has only bad memories of former Goon Show comic Michael Bentine who, when asked for his autograph in a restaurant, made a huge fuss to show how popular he was. Bentine refused to stay aboard and Mike had to sail to whichever hotel was nearest the next location. Once on board, Mike picked up two beer bottles and pretended to use them as binoculars. Bentine snatched them away and said: 'I'm the funnyman round here.'

Mike found it was easy to please his charterers as long as they were given plenty of sailing, not just round the estuary buoys and back. If it was possible to get away early on a Friday and the conditions were right, he would do Calais and back in a weekend.

'I think a good deal of the success in the venture lay in the fact that he is very easy-going and doesn't get worried about how they sailed his boat and doesn't shout,' said Kath. As far as family sailing was concerned, it worked well, for during a week or a long weekend with charterers he could generally get the boat down to the West Country or the Channel Islands, where Kath and the girls joined him. 'I liked this as he would have had his share of hard-bashing with the charterers and by the time we arrived he was content to do a little gentle coast hopping.' It was good timing as Kath had bought a pony and was returning to her beloved horse world and the children, now 10 and 11, did not want to go afloat every weekend.

Veronica remembers being sick quite often and she had grown to loathe being afloat. 'It was the classic "When are we going to stop?" and it was always round the next headland, round the next headland. My local schoolteacher said to me that I'd been to lots of places, but I said, "Yes, but only round the edges."'

A fire at the Fambridge boatyard gutted many yachts, but one of the FYC craft, *Concerto*, a Vertue although badly charred, had survived. Mike bought her as a project which made them a two-boat family, 'Well you've got two ponies,' he argued although one of Kath's steeds was just on loan. He had always admired Vertues, but could not justify keeping both craft and sold the Vertue to a sailor on the Solent. He delivered her there during a cold spell and regretted coveting her coal stove which he had removed to put in *Dowsabel* as it was fitted with heat radiating fins.

Mike's cartoons were now selling worldwide – from Holland and Germany to Japan: 'All they had to do was change the language of the captions,' he said. But to some extent he was a victim of his own success. Some shipmates were now nervous of sailing with him for fear of ending up as material. Boats which once sailed in company now tacked the other way when they saw *Dowsabel* coming. Mick Wilkins told me how one of the Flexible Yacht Club members had built a boat at Fambridge

"WOULD YOU LIKE A SPELL AT THE TILLER, DAVID?"

of teak instead of Douglas fir. 'When the tide came in it went right up past the waterline. She was twice the weight she should have been.' Everyone was there for the launch including Mike who inevitably turned the scenario into a cartoon. A figure in the drawing, standing on the slipway, says as the water rises nearer deck level: 'Soon be afloat now.' Mick recalls the DIY builder, who had recognised himself, bursting into the Ferry Boat one night in fury. 'I thought he was going to kill Mike,' he said.

Veronica, who now lives in a Victorian town house her parents bought in London's Stoke Newington, told me: 'Some of those cartoons I can remember straight from life. There was one where a yachtsman's wife was left hanging by a boathook from a harbour wall as the craft drifted out from the edge. Hilary and I thought it was terribly funny because she fell in the water.' This was Dallas, the former wife of Keith Waite, the fellow cartoonist mentioned earlier. Keith worked on national newspapers, including the Viscount Rothermere-owned *Daily Sketch*. It was while working on this title that Rothermere's son Vere Harmsworth, who managed the paper, came in to watch Keith working. The artist did not know who the chatty young fellow was and said: 'Look, mate, I don't quite know what you want, but I've got a deadline by four-thirty, so would you mind pissing off?' The gruff New Zealander became one of his boss's favourites after that. Keith, who lives in the East Coast sailing mecca Pin Mill, was more understanding of Mike's artistic licence than

"AND REMEMBER IN FUTURE YOU DON'T CHUCK THE BUCKET"

others who Mike sailed with: 'I used to enjoy his cartoons, he always amused me a lot,' he told me. And the legendary Carl Giles, whose post-war family graced the *Daily Express* for decades, and whose most famous character, grandma, has her own life-size statue in bronze on an Ipswich street, was also a fan of the Peyton style. Giles, who lived on his Suffolk farm and occasionally went sailing on the Orwell himself, told how he once went out with dinghy sailing legend Uffa Fox in which 'at least 50 Peyton calamities happened on that one short sail'. He added that: 'I like drawing sailing cartoons but nearly always abandon the idea because I know I could not make it funnier than Peyton. If I do draw one about boats, which is passably funny, I usually meet somebody who laughs then says: "Peyton did a beauty on that theme two or three years ago."'

Ian Griffiths, now 74 and himself a victim in the past, said: 'His cartoons are based on acute observation and an eye for the ludicrous. He has a prodigious memory for the telling throwaway remark, which often sums up a tense situation. Every work is related to an actual incident, which has happened to Mike or his long-suffering friends. Many yachtsmen will have seen or, dare I say it, had similar things happen to them.'

But one of the reasons Mike's charterers kept coming back was the amount of time they were allowed on the helm. As a result when things went wrong it was often because Mike was down below. Once, aboard *Touchstone*, she was squared away and running up Suffolk's River Ore past Havergate Island when the boom passed over the RSPB launch and then the mainsheet fouled the launch's radar scanner, tearing it off. 'The outcome was expensive,' said Ian, 'Mike could be sharp

THE COLDEST JUNE WEEK FOR SOME FIFTY ODD YEARS

when things went wrong.' He blew his top when *Dowsabel* was allowed to fall athwart the lock at Willemstad, Holland, and when Ian let the wrong end of a mooring line go at Ouistreham, France, and it jammed in the ring, 'he told me in no uncertain terms I should have known better. He was right and I have never done it since.' Ian, as an enlightened headmaster, recognised a teacher when he saw one and he found both Mike and Kath inspiring. 'They enriched my life. They opened up new horizons for me and gave me a completely different outlook on life,' he told me, 'Mike is very independent, very determined and never has the doubts some of us do. He is a tough cookie and takes things as they come. I remember sailing with him on *Dowsabel* once when he had charterers aboard. A leak meant that the only bedding he had which wasn't soaked was an old mainsail. He was quite happy with that wrapped round him in the cockpit.

'Also Mike always found enough time for the underdog, sometimes without much in return.'

Once aboard *Sugar Creek*, a youngster at the helm had got into an inextricable position between the smaller boat mooring trots at Burnham-on-Crouch. 'I think you'd better come up and take her,' the alarmed youngster yelled. Quickly sizing up the situation Mike realised there was no way out without hitting one other boat which he did. He brought up and left a note in the boat's cockpit accepting responsibility. The young helmsman was mortified, but Mike told him not to worry, 'We've all done it,' he said. Later that week Mike received mail from three different owners all claiming damage to their boats, which he had not been near. The one he had damaged he arranged to have taken up to Peter Pointer's yard for repair.

NOT LIKE THE WORK'S CANTEEN

Although she was only a 'pottering cruiser' Mike was amazed to find three sextants down below!

Mike never wasted timber on his boats and not one of them had a loo door. Once, aboard *Dowsabel*, Jimmy Green was using the head and noticed that the discharge pipe was clear plastic. As he flushed he told the gathered company: 'Same old crap on TV tonight.'

In *Touchstone*, Mike had often cut 25 miles off his passage to the Medway and its creeks by negotiating the shoal route through Havengore and across the Maplin Sands. Before the bridge-keeper got to know the boat he was concerned she wouldn't get over the 3 miles of hard sand and called down to ask Mike's draught. Mike showed him three fingers for her 3 feet of hull beneath the waterline, but even so on many occasions she has 'stirred the sand astern and bumped across the Broomway'; this is the ancient low tide road across the sands, which is the highest point.

Any local skipper knows that once you are over that you are also over the worst. But new charterers were agog to think there was 3 miles more before deep water could be reached.

Long Acre was no longer the arcadia it once had been. South Woodham Ferrers was transforming from a shanty town built on muddy tracks to a new town of expensive, individually designed, brick-built houses on metalled roads. These houses, complete with walled gardens and streets lined with new saplings, had stretched nearer and nearer the Peyton cottage and were now nudging their boundary and 'were about to overtake us on the other side of the road'. It was time to move on.

In 1968 Kath had scored a major success with her 12th novel *Flambards*, about an unhappy teenage girl who takes solace in her horses. It was the first of a trilogy and would be made into a TV series by Yorkshire Television. It was hugely popular and is still available and sold regularly on DVD.

Kath was now a well-recognised author with awards from the American Library Association (Best Books for Young Adults), *The New York Herald Tribune*, *The Boston Globe*, *The Guardian*, and was a Carnegie Medal winner. However, despite her achievements she recalls attending a literary supper in London when a young man sat down beside her and said: 'I understand you are married to Mike Peyton?'

So between them there was now the money to buy a property with some land. They found Rookery Cottage, then a semi-detached, two up and two down, with a bath in the kitchen and a bucket down the garden for a loo. Kath refused to move in until it was improved, and Mike told her she had lost her pioneering spirit. 'I took a tape measure down to the cottage and found that I could get my piano in although it meant climbing over the arm of the sofa to get up the stairs.' But the clincher was the fact it had 5 acres, plus another 5 that they bought from a farmer, and moved Mike's boat junk and Kath's horses there. Although it was a longer walk to the river, once more they would be surrounded by fields and muddy tracks. The day of the

move, Mike was away on a delivery job and just to remind her, as Kath dealt with the demands of uprooting everything from South Woodham Ferrers, a postcard arrived from Stromboli. 'You can guess how I felt about that, but Mike has always done exactly what he wants, regardless. Mostly I go along with it because he allows me the same freedom, but just sometimes...I see other wives being "cherished" – that is the lovely word – but Mike just laughs. I have to be very near death to find out that he loves me.'

Rookery Cottage is a very different place to the streets of Stoke Newington. The night I went to meet Veronica I caught a bus up the Holloway Road –

Kath with horse and hound, Rookery Cottage

she had been working recently as a librarian in the eponymous female prison – and asked the driver, as the 73 swayed speedily north, where Milton Grove was. He thought for a minute and gave me directions: 'It's behind a new estate. If you go right to the end, you'll pass a synagogue on your left and a burned out pub opposite. Ask again there.'

I wandered the empty back streets and found the landmarks accompanied by the barking of a throaty dog, the wail of a faraway siren and the persistent ringing of an ignored burglar alarm. A young African in chef's clothing left the kitchen of a café to point me in the right direction and eventually I found myself atop a high stoop ringing the bell of an imposing black door.

A dark-haired woman let me in and we climbed steep stairs to a dimly lit room full of cigarette smoke with black painted walls, bare floorboards and book-lined alcoves. Veronica had inherited the spartanism of her father and the cheekbones of her mother.

'Dad's boats were usually quite minimalist,' she said, drawing on a cigarette, 'but he always got the fire sorted. Everybody had fairly crummy old boats in those early days and they were obsessive about them. They sailed every weekend. Now they are packed in marinas like floating caravans.'

What had life been like for a teenage girl living miles from anywhere? 'I remember walking enormous distances in platform shoes...to Maldon and Danbury. But they cut us a lot of slack as long as they knew where we were. The very nice thing about dad was that he encouraged us to have our own careers in a time when girls just grew up and got married, despite women's lib, which took a long time to filter down...'

As I left Veronica's home I noticed a calendar of black and white photographs taken of the East Coast by marine photographer Den Phillips hanging on the kitchen wall.

'A reminder of home?' I asked.

'Yes, but too much racing and not enough marsh and mud this year,' she said. Veronica might not have taken to sailing – though she has done enough of it – but as far as the Thames Estuary goes she is a Peyton through and through.

Hilary, blond, did inherit her father's love of sailing. She lives with her husband, German-born Axel Mehnert in what was once a brick-built barn at the back of Rookery Cottage and is now converted to a home, but still with owl boxes in the roof.

She remembers South Woodham Ferrers well: 'There were funny, old people living in railway carriages and we lived among them with no TV and no car. Our parents were a bit bohemian and people thought we were odd. It was a little piece of land in a lost world bordered by the railway line and the creeks. The lane was lined with enormous elms, behind which stood cornfields which ran down to the grassy sea wall where there were little raised sloe thickets, where we had picnics in summer. We did have an idyllic childhood: to have had that freedom in that safe little world.

'Now you can't even see the contours of the place. It has completely gone. The sea wall is a place of urban dog-walking with a fake park nearby.'

Other development feared by the Clements Green Creekers had been the Magnox nuclear power station at Bradwell-on-Sea, very much part of the Essex sailor's world. Construction began on the Dengie Peninsula in 1957 and Mike was anchored in *Vagrant* when he was witness to an astonishing sight. Power station workers turned

Kath and Mike at Rookery Cottage in the Essex marshlands

up with a tug towing a boiler they needed to get up the boat-congested creek. 'It was a weekday and nobody was about. They hooked up all the anchored boats and plucked them out bodily from the sea-bed then dragged the whole lot – anchors, boats and all – out of the way. Now there would be endless litigation, he told me.

Today Bradwell power station invites a certain amount of affection from the mariner, its giant glass cubes are a navigation mark which can be seen by day or night. They have a solitary high-tech majesty surrounded by something as primeval as marsh, mud and wildfowl.

'When we all moaned about its coming we never suspected that it might show us great beauty,' Kath said. 'Every facet of glass and concrete throws back the sunrise; a sharp-edged, short-lived pattern of fireworks against the greyness of the early morning.'

Mike and Kath had by now both made a financial success of their very individual ways of life. They bought a third property in Spain and a cottage on the Guadiana River on the Portuguese border. Mike no longer needed to be within a 50 mile radius of London as the magazines now chased him for work which he could send via the post, and Kath could write books anywhere. The moors of their youth did not lure them back up north.

As Kath summed it up:

'We had learnt our sailing in the Thames Estuary, and we still find it strange at times to touch bottom with the boathook when out of sight of land. It is an odd, ugly but endearing cruising ground with its short ochre seas and cormorant-topped beacons. At night there are areas – like the Edinburgh Channel – ablaze with light like an aircraft landing strip; but sometimes, when making one's way from buoy to buoy by compass in thick weather, the very names on the chart from Gunfleet to Goodwins with their associations of wreck and disaster, do nothing to soothe the peering anxiety of the helmsman, aware of the ultimate half-inch of draught beneath him.

'The Essex shore, from its urban emergence out of London on the north shore of the Thames, all the way via Foulness, Dengie, Mersea, Clacton, Frinton and Walton to Harwich where it meets Suffolk, is a poor, inconspicuous thing, blue and faint beyond the mud flats, its thin withies standing up forlorn, its nearest approach to a cliff is the crumbling earthy Naze at Walton, all 200 feet of it. Small wonder that 'foreigners' from the West Country and the Solent rarely broach the difficulties of the estuary for such small return. The traffic is all the other way, the ditch-crawlers of Essex seeking the yachting paradises they read about in the magazines. We go away every summer, and have used the Solent many times as a jumping off ground for points farther on, but always on our return, rounding the Whitaker beacon and starting the long beat back into the utterly flat horizon that we know to be the mouth of the River Crouch, we feel a warm sense of affection for our home ground: its landscape of nothingness, the puzzles of its swatchways that we think we have begun to master, its thick water sliding out of salting and ditch where the waders cry with their queer night calls...

'We have seen it in most of its moods, from drifting along with the tide in a summer heat-haze to abandoning ship when it bared its teeth one unpleasant April, and we would not swap our home base at Fambridge for any more fulsome, picturesque mooring. The guidebooks do not bother much with Fambridge, and rightly. It does not 'nestle in trees at the water's edge' nor lie in a 'picturesque sprawl'. The wind whistles across its marshes even in the height of summer, for there is nothing to stop it, and there are times when one cannot even get aboard at high water, when a good wind and a spring tide are fighting it out, even though it is twelve miles inland.

'It has a businesslike road to the water's edge, a hard, a boatyard and a pub, which is all one needs. It also has two old cottages, the nearest to the water, which have plugs in the living room floor which one can pull out when necessary to let out the tide...'

The East Coast had claimed them.

· 18 ·

The Boat Show

Among the eager, open and animated faces pressed against the window of the Disney-like Docklands Light Railway train was one expressionless visage unnoticed in the crowd. Mike Peyton had come among his subjects for the annual pilgrimage to the London Boat Show. The doors hissed open and the train passengers, dressed in deck shoes and sailing jackets, poured out in their hundreds onto Custom House station. The ExCel sign glowed over their heads in the cold January sky and, chattering confidently to one another, they flowed en masse up the covered walkway their ears assaulted by the oikey ticket touts, their nostrils prickling at the coal smoke of the chestnut cookers. It was a remnant of Dickensian London among the monied spires of the new satellite capital. Inside this mecca of marine materialism sat the glossy new boats encapsulated in carpeted stairways worthy of Bruce Forsyth's descent. At the feet of these gleaming beasts, with the potential for world girdling, the anoraked multitude opined with the dedication of the uncommitted window-shopper then go off and drown their covetousness in Guinness.

I had arranged with the ladies dressed in the Oyster corporate uniforms for Mike to board the most expensive boat at the show: the Oyster 65, a snip at £2 million. 'It's immoral,' he said, and then as he pulled on elasticated overshoes, 'It's like going into a mosque...but the only reason I'm putting these on is because I've got a hole in my sock.' Down below in the immaculately finished saloon, earnest-looking visitors in reefer jackets and exclusively striped ties sat talking quietly, and seriously, with more Oyster uniforms, this time worn by men. The only thing we had in common with them were the elasticated slippers. No one appeared to notice us, although the serious discussions halted momentarily when Mike, who had been rooting around forward of the mast support, said: 'There's room for one here.'

'What?' I asked.

'A coal stove.'

When told by an Oyster man that the boat was fitted with a Perkins diesel, Mike said mysteriously, 'That's good, all the taxis in Europe have Perkins, or did have, so it's handy for spares.'

Back on deck, Mike noticed the varnished cockpit table, 'The only varnish on my boat is the tiller,' he said and then as the salesman showed him the table included a fridge, added: 'I remember once we were sailing in Greece in my concrete boat *Lodestone*. We didn't have a cockpit table, but strange to say a piece of flotsam drifted by with four legs sticking up: it was a table. We had our lunch on it then threw it back in.'

Totting up our finances I reckoned we still could not afford an Oyster 65 even if we sold both our houses and pooled the money. Mike turned to *Yachting Monthly* photographer Graham Snook, who was accompanying us, and said 'Do you want to come in?'

'It's immoral,' Mike said about the £2 million cost

A Perkins diesel – great for taxi spares

'I haven't got a house,' said Graham and we climbed back down to earth in the form of the exhibition hall sea-bed effect carpet.

Later at lunch in the RYA exhibitors lounge, we shared a table with a smartly suited man of easy demeanour who turned out to be a City financier who also did not recognise Mike. Once I introduced them, our dining companion, who sat on my right, talked nine-to-the-dozen across my plate to Mike who sat on my left. Mike stared blankly back, carefully masticating and wordless.

'Well it's been a privilege to have broken bread with you,' said the man as we left.

'Oh for Christ's sake,' said Mike. Uncertain if, in this context, that was blasphemous or not, I smiled as though our fellow diner had not heard the remark, but I knew he had.

Mike first attended the Boat Show many years ago when he was seeking ideas for replacing *Dowsabel* which was too small for chartering. He wandered around the Earls Court halls like so many before him, seeking the perfect boat. 'I'd looked at all the forty footers at the show and was disappointed. There was one which boasted having an "international designer" but he seemed concerned only with scatter cushions.' None of the GRP production boats included his own eccentricities; a wooden boat would be too expensive so, to eradicate the perceived failings of all his craft, he decided to build one himself. That's when he discovered ferro-cement and the fact that a designer on his doorstep at Burnham-on-Crouch, had been broad-minded enough to accept commissions for ferro-cement boats at a time when many thought it was beneath them. And so the paths of Mike Peyton and Alan F Hill crossed.

There were those at Fambridge who also thought ferro-cement beneath them. One was wooden boat enthusiast Gordon Hamilton, who told me: 'Mike disappeared into cement which we all thought was a disaster.'

But there were others who saw its potential: Jimmy Green fitted a GRP deck and cabin onto a concrete hull he'd acquired; Ian Griffiths built a ferro-boat so big he entered the Tall Ships race in her; and Mick Wilkins turned his bricklaying skills

'Where's the comb and scissors?' 'We once found a cockpit table floating by'

into 'plastering' expertise and built many. He became famous throughout the Solent as well as the East Coast for his knowledge and lives on a concrete boat to this day.

Lodestone was built in the grounds of Rookery Cottage. Kath can still point to the spot. They were not good times for her. 'He wouldn't talk...he completely ignored me and the children, so stressed out was he over this boat. Blokes turned up from all over the country on weekends to talk about concrete boats. It was awful – I almost divorced him.' Mike also fell out with a shipwright who had agreed to do a job, but then dropped his project when a bigger contract came along. 'Once someone has offended him he cuts you off. He didn't talk to that man for 30 years. Mike has no forgiveness...that's a wart for your biography, put that down,' Kath told me as Mike sat uncomfortably in the cottage kitchen one day.

'What made the whole thing such a nightmare was that Mike insisted on putting a deadline on the date the boat must be launched and absolutely sticking to it,' said Kath, 'It was one year to sail away. Bloody ridiculous. No wonder he was in such a vile temper all the time.' It didn't help matters that Hilary was doing her O-levels and Kath was writing to a deadline as well: to produce 75,000 words that year.

Mike took his ideas to Alan Hill:

'I wanted a 40 ft boat with a small cockpit, flush deck, buoyant transom with a stern-hung rudder and a dog house with a chart table big enough to unfold an Admiralty chart. Beneath that I wanted room for an air cooled Lister 44 hp diesel with a hand start. She must be shoal draught – no more than four feet with the centre-board raised – and this would be housed in the saloon table. She needed to sleep eight: two in quarter berths, two in the forepeak and three in the saloon and one in the pilot berth. My berth would be in the dog house next to the chart table and near the cockpit. She would need to be yawl rigged; the more string for charterers to pull the better. For the same reason – keeping charterers occupied – she would need to be labour intensive and set a mizzen staysail. She would have no echo-sounder, instead a leadline would be swung. The cabin would be as large as possible as parties were popular with customers and there must be a coal stove. To eradicate extra through-hull holes there would be a bucket and chuck-it head. The mast would be stepped on a tabernacle with cap shrouds on hinges so it could be lowered under control. There would be no anchor windlass as there would always be plenty of charterers to hoick up the pick...'

Up in Alan Hill's design office along the Burnham road, he scratched his head and told me: 'There was no finesse, he wanted these big, nuggety features and a stubby rudder: he had this obsession with barges and smacks...I mean I was brought up by Robert Clark.'

Mike punned: 'All he had to do was put it down on paper and turn it into something concrete.'

Mike's stubbornness for his deadline paid off. Jimmy Green died before his boat was complete. Ian's took eight years, but Mike sailed away on the date decided. 'He wanted us to go with him and I said you can't take Hilary in her O-level year. He didn't understand this: he said she could take it next year! I was incoherent with rage,' said Kath.

The day came for *Lodestone*'s maiden voyage and Alan joined the proud owner as they cast off from the Fambridge mooring. 'The wind was south-easterly and I was on the helm. Whatever I did she kept luffing up towards the south wall...the weather helm was horrible.' He discovered that friction on the stock was causing the rudder to come up. This was sorted out and after that she sailed well. Something good had come out of the union: around a dozen *Lodestone*s were built.

Now Mike threw down the bait to trap his family into coming away during the Easter Holiday: Paris! But that year there was a barge strike on the French canals and 'Paris ha ha, we got stopped in the coalfields of northern France. It was snowing, there was no stove on board; the drinking water tasted of epoxy resin and made me ill,' said Kath. She took the girls back to Essex. 'How I hated him,' she said.

Mike took *Lodestone* through 200 locks and through nearly 800 miles of canal and river from Calais to the Med. In one of the locks *Lodestone* got nipped between the closing gates when her concrete topsides came into their own. Mike carried on sometimes with crew, sometimes alone. His family re-joined him for visits to Cannes, and St Tropez, where Kath arrived to find a topless girl on board. Fortunately for Mike she was the target of legless sailor Tristan Jones, who the cartoonist met on the French Riviera. They also sailed to Sardinia and Corsica, where both Kath and Mike – on a later visit – laced up their hiking boots once more and crossed the island over its peaks on a 17 day hike.

Mike brought *Lodestone* back to England via the Canal du Midi and the Gironde where, having entered the Bay of Biscay, he was sailing once more. From Ushant to Falmouth he discovered the boat would sail herself under just mizzen and headsail with a beam wind in a blow: 'Our watches were spent sitting in the dog house and we never needed oilskins as we did not touch the helm or sheets once for 100 miles. I have never had a sail remotely like it since.'

From Falmouth Mike port hopped east single-handed until 'Rounding the North Foreland was like coming home. Perhaps the sun did not shine so much, perhaps the sea wasn't blue and clear but these were home waters and they were appreciated all the more for my having sailed elsewhere.'

He was by now well established as the leading yachting cartoonist anywhere in the world. He was now producing greetings cards for the Met Office, but his exposure in the British yachting press had led to commissions in their foreign counterparts such as the German *Die Yacht*, the French *Voiles et Voiliers* and the Dutch *Waterkampioen*. It was his work in the latter which had an unexpected impact. Ian Griffiths was cruising in Norway when he and his wife befriended a couple who had sailed there from Holland. When their new friends discovered Ian was an East Coaster, they said: 'We never come to the Thames Estuary because of all the dreadful things that happen there. We've seen them in the cartoons.' They would rather risk the fjords of such a wild coastline than the much nearer horizon of adjacent Essex, thanks to the very believable catastrophes drawn by Mike. For *Voiles et Voiliers*, who commissioned him to sail around Brittany producing cartoons, Mike felt it was such a good job that he sent back

Yachting Monthly cover August 1979, Kath lying on the beach with *Lodestone* in background

part of his advanced expenses. It was still being talked about in their head office decades later! When the editors of these journals realised he actually sailed to get the material, he was also asked to write as well. He was flown to Levkas, Greece, for the Peyton take on the fledgling concept of flotilla sailing. For the Sail Training Association's journal he shipped aboard their topsail schooner *Winston Churchill* for a North Sea passage in a Force 10 blow, the heaviest weather Mike has ever had to face. He went to Chesapeake Bay to do a special book for the American market, *Hurricane Zoë and Other Sailing*. This was not a success: 'The book sold better in Germany than in the US because in America they felt I was laughing at them instead of with them,' Mike told me, 'one cartoon I did had a yachtsman calling up the Coastguard for ice. The fact that they actually do that meant it wasn't funny to them.'

Mike had another sideline – painting portraits of owners' boats. 'I used to paint the sea first,' he told me, 'they could pick their own sea…if they wanted a Force 6 they could have it, then I'd paint the boat in.'

Through Kath's passion for horses and horse riding – she was now a member of the local hunt – Mike also penned cartoons for *Horse & Hound*. His ill-fated black and white characters were in demand too for a new pub guide, and he became a good friend of its author, Hungarian-born gourmet Egon Ronay, who would take him for lunch at London's exclusive Gay Hussar restaurant. 'He was such a big wheel there they'd almost cut the food up and put it in your mouth,' Mike told me. He wanted to return his host's hospitality and invite him down to Rookery Cottage, but Kath was horrified. Though her casseroles, continually bubbling on the stove, were popular with the Clements Green Creekers, fresh off the frozen marsh, and a man who would eat anything that

Mike sailing in the Med

could be digested, Kath did not believe her diners had discriminating palates and vetoed the Ronay visit. Their association continued, however, and between them they also produced Castrol branded road maps.

Though Hilary had become a natural sailor her parents weren't too happy when in the summer of 1974 she announced she was joining a group of hippies aboard a concrete boat bound from Burnham-on-Crouch to British Columbia. But, as ever, they did not 'cramp her style' as the phrase of the time described enlightened parenting. However on the night she left, a storm blew up in the Thames Estuary and English Channel and they were worried sick, especially when the next day's news included the loss of Prime Minister Edward Heath's *Morning Cloud III* along with two crew, including her owner's godson, Christopher Chadd, on a delivery trip back to the Solent after racing at...Burnham-on-Crouch. They were hugely relieved when Hilary called to say they were in Calais, that of the six-strong crew only she and one other could sail, and that the voyage had been abandoned. Hilary went on to cross the Atlantic on a delivery trip in a Beneteau 50 from Nice to Barbados with Frank Mulville's son Adrian. On another transatlantic delivery trip, while moored at La Graciosa, Hilary met her husband Axel Mehnert, crewing on another yacht. But she still recalls the first time she took the helm of a boat aboard *Sugar Creek*: 'Dad went below and let me take the boat through the moorings at Fambridge, while he watched from the cabin.'

After seven years successful chartering with *Lodestone*, Mike decided to expand his 'fleet' and ordered a second concrete boat from Alan Hill. *Brimstone* a 35 ft, yawl-rigged centre-boarder, was born. An inquiry into the loss of *Morning Cloud* revealed that her washboards had dropped out when she was knocked down and she subsequently had swamped. Acting on this, Mike over-reacted and did away with the normal companionway and instead to enter *Brimstone* you had to hop up on the bridgedeck and lower yourself down through a hole in the cabin top. 'It was safe but inconvenient,' Mike confessed. Both boats would now charter in company, but their proprietor soon discovered that trying to find an experienced skipper to take the second boat, plus all the extra maintenance and book-keeping, was going against the whole concept of his life: namely that he worked to live and not the other way round. He told me: 'I thought Giles' cartoons were fantastic – he'd got it made – but I did not want to go to town every day, like he did at first, I'd rather earn less and go sailing.'

Mike had designed his life and was sticking to it.

But before he sold *Brimstone* both boats made a memorable estuary trip to the Red Sand Towers. The Red Sands, along with their sisters the Shivering Sand Towers, were built during World War 2 as anti-aircraft platforms and still stand like ominous *War of the World*-like structures to this day. It is impossible to get on them

PEYTON

"THEY WANT TO KNOW IF WE'VE GOT THE 'EAST SUNK' ON BOARD"

any more as their hanging ladders have been cut away by engineers sent from the MOD worried they'd face expensive litigation. But the rusting rungs were still there when Mike and one of his regular charterers, Geoff Cox from the Frampton Sailing Club in Gloucestershire climbed 60 ft up for a look. They had to use the sides of the rungs as they were so rotten and on the 'spidery walkways above we left footprints as though in snow: except it was rust'.

For many years Mike had hankered after 'doing a Fastnet;' he knew it was not his cup of tea, but also that it would supply him with cartoon ideas for years. His chance came when Kath bumped into John Puxley in Burnham one day. He was the son of the man from whom Mike had bought his first boat, *Vagrant*. John told Kath he was off to race in the Fastnet on a local boat, *Trophy*, an Oyster 37, designed by Holman & Pye. Their eight-strong crew were one member short, would Mike like to fill the berth?

Mike was frustrated: there was no way he could join the race as he had other commitments. This was the storm-smashed 1979 Fastnet when 15 yachtsmen died from drowning or hypothermia and 20 yachts were abandoned, several of which sank. Three of *Trophy*'s crew, including John, 42, died after the liferaft they had climbed into split apart.

Mike never did 'do' a Fastnet.

• 19 •

Cartoon into Boat

Awiry figure with a roll of cartridge paper under his arm crunched up the driveway of Alan Hill's Burnham-on-Crouch home. It was the spring of 1981.

'"Eh look at this," Mike said to me, unrolling this sheet of paper. Here was this image of some sort of boat. The mast was out of scale, the rudder too big,' recalled Alan laughing, 'he wanted it as light as possible, with a round bilge, a flat bottom, twin drop boards which would be hoisted and lowered with a block and tackle rigged to the mast. He wanted her flat on the inside, shaped on the outside. It was purely experimental.'

Tony Robinson said: 'Alan would throw his hands up in the air when Mike turned up. He is not practical at all, but he is an ideas man.' Once again Alan's palms went heavenwards, but Mike is stubborn, he persisted and *Touchstone*, a 38 ft concrete ketch, was born. 'Designing his boat was like bringing a cartoon to life,' Alan told me. 'She had an extremely heavy bottom with 10 meshes of steel in it and 8 inch deep floors which, before we poured in the concrete, were filled with anything Mike could get his hands on including, I remember, a discarded frying pan.' Mike disputes this: a frying pan was far too valuable an object to commit to ballast! The concreting of the bilges was carried out once the hull was afloat so that the boat could be trimmed to her marks: a simple but revolutionary idea of Mike's. 'In his crude way he had some good ideas,' admitted Alan, although he did not agree with all of them.

Mike wanted a cambered deck and when he discovered this meant that all the deck beams would have to be designed individually to fit, rather like the bones of a fish, and that this would be time-consuming and expensive, he ordered Alan to run the deck beams longitudinally. The hands went into supplication mode once more. But lengthwise they became. The sides were much lighter than the bottom, with only half the amount of steel and the decks of light plywood. This kept the centre of gravity low. Another practical idea of Mike's was to leave the fitting of the grabrails down below until she'd been sailed with charterers aboard several times. 'Then we placed them where the handprints were.'

The drop boards were aerofoiled – like those of *Clementine*. Mike had noticed how the Dutch had made this sophisticated improvement to their lee-boards, unlike the Thames barges which, apart from a few later, racy exceptions, did not. They are angled inwards a few degrees which helps her performance to windward. Alan wanted a system of hydraulics to lift the daggers, Mike did not, he wanted them on tackles as he knew the huge value of giving charterers a rope to pull on. It made them feel part of the crew. However after raising and lowering these heavy daggers after a few tacks, some wished they were just passengers again.

The mast is stepped in a mast-case – like a Thames barge – and can be raised and lowered by taking a bolt out of its heel. The cap shroud chain plates are fitted to a

Mike in his chart-lined study at Rookery Cottage

triangular device each side – another idea gleaned from *Clementine* – so that they act as guy ropes when the mast is being lowered or raised to steady the rig. As a result Mike can carry out the operation single-handed.

Her rig was brilliantly described by Ian Griffiths as being a 'bermudian gaffer' and one day, who knows, the 'baffer' rig may come about. *Touchstone* has a tall mast which sets a bermudian sail, but she also has another rig which uses a gaff to supply a topsail. When reefed it is the foot of the mainsail which gets shortened – again as smacks and bawleys do when tricing the main. Keeping the topsail up, with the mainsail gone – as Thames barges do – gives her performance to windward, which traditional gaffers do not have once they are reefed in the conventional way. It was Mike's hybrid imagination, cross-breeding a Thames barge with a modern day yacht with her fully battened main, which produced this mind-boggling rig. She had a crank handle for the engine which extended into the saloon so that four charterers could hand start it!

Aviva, Open 60. They may be carbon-fibre but these dagger boards had already been 'invented' by Mike for *Touchstone*

• 149 •

Alan Hill 'Designing Mike's boat was like bringing a cartoon to life'

Alan Hill on piano. Relaxing from the stress of Mike's ideas

'After his first sail in a blow Mike rang me up and asked "How big an angle should the boat go over?" I told him 40 degrees maximum. "Oh, we went over much further than that," he told me proudly. I held my breath. "But we came back again."'

Alan put the phone down and went back to playing Debussy on the piano in his design office, to sooth his nerves. 'It's just as well he's a good sailor and doesn't get into a flap,' he told me.

Mike later told Alan that all the money he spent with the designer he got back with the multiple ideas he had for cartoons which came from the 'building, the commissioning and all the things that went wrong along the way!'

Brimming with confidence at his skills with concrete, Mike now built his wife a mounting block: three steps of cement so she could get on her horse. It has stood the test of time well and, hidden near the garage, has left more than one guest with a visit to the panel beaters.

It was while sailing *Lodestone* that the most important design-wrinkle, adopted later in the building of *Touchstone*, was born. *Lodestone* was sailing in the mouth of the Blackwater when one of the charterers noticed a woman on all fours scampering forward on the deck of a yacht which was out of control. The boat had gybed, her boom injuring and knocking a crewman overboard. Because he was unconscious the skipper had dropped the headsail, and fired up the engine before diving to the rescue. The headsail sheet had then wrapped round the prop, leaving an inexperienced wife, single-handed. She had been trying to disentangle the sheet when *Lodestone* arrived to hear the horror story. Both men drowned: the crewman because he was unconscious and the skipper because he could not get back aboard. Mike and crew did what they could to help and searched unsuccessfully for the missing sailors. Mike later built *Touchstone* with a simple step on the trailing edge of her transom-hung rudder. It has saved the lives of two of Mike's charterers over the years: one a diabetic who had a collapse and went overboard, the other a man who fell over while relieving

Touchstone gaff-rigged Bermudian ketch

Touchstone sailing for a honeymoon couple

himself from the stern sheets. 'I think all boats with transom-hung rudders should have a step included in the moulding,' Mike said, 'it is a simple but effective life-saver.'

During one winter charter up the River Colne, some of Mike's regulars spotted a glistening creek entrance opposite Wivenhoe. 'Where's that go?' one asked. 'That's the Roman River,' said Mike, and *Touchstone*'s bow sheered to port as they started up the twisting Fingringhoe Creek which leads to an old mill, once served by sailing barges, but which had been out of operation for years by the time of *Touchstone*'s approach. Mike was down below stoking the fire when there was a rending crash and the boat jerked.

Up on deck an acrid smell arrested his nostrils and looking up he found the top third of his aluminium mast had burnt off having hit overhead electric cables. 'Everyone of the crew was a Yachtmaster, they were all boat-owners themselves,' Mike told me, 'but not one of them spotted it'. When Mike reported to his insurance broker that it was going to cost £900 to re-sleeve the mast he got the unforgettable reply: 'That's the least of my worries, I've got a quarter of a million claim from the local hospital and a supermarket and an industrial estate because they were cut off, too!'

One of the Yachtmasters was Peter Maynard, a chartered accountant. Peter was a very different kind of sailor to the mud-bespattered Clements Green Creekers. There were no boiler suits for him. He was more likely to be wearing a neckerchief and a Guernsey jumper. He was one of what Mike described as the 'Maldon set'. Affable, intelligent and good-humoured, he liked fine wines and fine boats: he had owned an Albert Strange cutter, a Folkboat and a Colchester smack.

Mike had now moved *Touchstone* from his native River Crouch to the neighbouring River Blackwater, to Maldon itself where she was moored in a mud-berth at Downs Boatyard. This was because he had joined a syndicate of 11 buyers, including Alan Hill, Arthur Keeble and John Dines, father of the current proprietor, Jim, who purchased the yard for £5,000 each, to prevent it being developed into riverside property.

Being moored permanently alongside was more convenient for getting charterers aboard and as Mike went up and down the river, passing the esplanade each time, he did not realise that buried beneath it was the hulk of the old *Lancashire*, Tubby Blake's 'yacht', as she was once known, aboard which he and Kath had spent a night on their honeymoon. She had been used to plug a hole in the sea wall before being covered in landfill.

Peter Maynard's wife Jo struck up a friendship with Kath and all four went away together on *Touchstone*. The boys sailed the boat down to Brittany and the girls cycled there, joining the boat for the return trip, their bicycles lashed to the pushpit.

As we sat in the book-lined study of his imposing early Victorian detached home on the top of the hill in Maldon, Peter told me he found it hard to reconcile Mike's makeshift approach to sailing with his own Yachtmaster learnt ways. It was good of him to see me at such short notice as he wanted to settle down and watch the Five Nations Rugby tour on TV.

'Maintenance was just not in Mike's vocabulary, he wants to fix everything with a piece of string. I remember we were down in Douarnenez and the bilge pump started playing up. I suggested the French chandlers did a nice little pump for £50, but Mike ignored me and carried on rooting around in his lockers until he found an old baked bean tin and fixed it with that. He also doesn't like spending money in marinas and will always anchor off. I remember being anchored about 2 miles off Boulogne with extra warps bent to the anchor cable. We had to stand watch as we were still in the inshore shipping lanes. He was lucky having charterers all year round as there would always be one who left behind his jacket, so Mike never had to buy one himself.'

Despite Mike's mend and make-do approach to sailing he, Peter and *The Guardian* journalist David Fairhall combined talents to write, film and produce an instructional video, *Pass Your Yachtmaster's*.

Peter once rafted up alongside *Touchstone* in the Pyefleet and with his crew stepped aboard to join Mike, who was sailing solo, for supper. The air temperature was keen and they were grateful to huddle round Mike's coal stove. As they waited for the stew to cook their hunger drove them to recall the best meal they'd ever had. Peter could never forget the wild strawberries in white wine vinegar he had at Hedges & Butler in London's Mayfair. His crew remembered the lobster thermidor on jasmine rice in Suffolk's Seckford Hall. 'We then both turned to Mike, who'd sat listening quietly. And he said "The best meal I ever had was Alsatian in a POW camp."'

Jo came in with tea at this point and said: 'He'll eat anything; any old rubbish, and go back for seconds...and thirds. He can go to sleep at the drop of a hat: "It's petrol in the tank," he'll say.'

Mike could have joined the others with a swanky boast about an illustrious meal: he had eaten at London's exclusive Athenaeum Club in Pall Mall, the guest of Sidney Chapman, where he met Sir Geoffrey Ingram Taylor, the Cambridge mathematician and yachtsman who invented the CQR anchor. But the stewed dog was a much better story and Mike – in true journalist style – liked lobbing the odd hand-grenade in polite company.

During Mike's early days chartering he met a young Swiss student, Carlo Metzler, who was on an English school exchange living with a family in Maldon during the

Carlo Metzler and new bride Barbara with Mike and friends aboard *Touchstone*

summer of 1978. While on a sailing trip with the English family he had met Mike on a chartering trip in *Lodestone*. After a raft up and lunch Carlo had been press-ganged into helping paint Mike's new vessel, *Brimstone*.

The young man returned to Switzerland full of stories about this amazing flat place called Essex where these amazing people lived near a sea wall and sailed boats made out of concrete. A long-distance friendship built up and the Peytons were invited to stay with Carlo's family in Cari in the Swiss Alps. Overjoyed at being among the mountains again, Mike wanted to 'go native' and spend the night sleeping in a snow hole instead of the chalet Carlo had booked for the week's skiing. After one night sleeping out he had to be dissuaded by Carlo who warned that the weather was warming up and there was a danger of an avalanche. Mike's imagination was soon at work and the trips became regular. Sometimes he went on his own, sometimes he took Veronica, or Kath, occasionally he went with the 'Maldon set' – all members of the Maldon Little Ship Club – but he learnt how to ski and more importantly how to capture people on skis fouling up.

Tony Robinson remembers going on one ski trip with Mike and Kath to Val d'Isère. 'I thought it was a suicidal black run – the steepest of the lot. I cursed him. "You bloody fool," I said. But it didn't bother him; he faced it the same as he faced sailing. We got down all right – mostly on our bottoms.' And Peter Maynard recalls another terrifying run he once made with Mike when a blizzard blew so hard it

Mike got cartoon ideas in the Alps

Peter and Jo Maynard at their home in Maldon, Essex

stopped them mid-slope, then the wind eased and they carried on down. But it had 'broken their fall' at the right time and they came to no harm. Carlo's mother became a legend with the Maldon set for her cooking, but when Mike had a gall bladder operation he was told not to eat cream. 'He took no notice and was in such appalling pain he ended up back in hospital,' Peter recalls.

Now he had a new line of cartoons and figures hurtling out of control at greater speeds than yachts would take them. 'Everyone has a different way of skiing and dad took this and exaggerated it, but he doesn't do caricatures,' said Veronica. Through ski hut windows, hanging for dear life on cable cars, or out-running an avalanche these learners on the ski slopes provided a rich vein of humour. One included two novices atop a very steep slope about to set off with one asking the other: 'What comes after "Our Father who art in heaven"?' This was a repeat of a similar predicament he had created for a horseman at an ominous jump, but which had caused letters of complaint from *Horse & Hound* magazine readers. With the legendary sexual shenanigans that went on off piste, Mike reckoned skiers were God-less enough to risk this particular cartoon again. There were no complaints.

Carlo became a successful dentist and married, taking his bride Barbara for their honeymoon aboard *Touchstone* in 1987:

> With a broken down engine, only the three of us on board with a very heavy topsail and no winches, having to tow the heavy boat by oars from the dinghy we set off. Mike said that with charterers he would have fixed the engine, but with friends he would sail like in the old days. So, our honeymoon voyage involved no engine, no marinas, only anchoring in the rivers, and never knowing if wind and tide would do the trick or not. It was hard work and great fun and Mike said if we could put up with this we could put up with the rest of our married life...

Soon other members of the Swiss connection were arriving in Essex to see what all the fuss was about. Carlo's younger brother, Lorenzo, came over to learn English aboard and was soon swearing with a northern accent, especially during a Boxing Day passage to the Humber when they ran for shelter in a northerly blow into Wells, the dangerous bar of which they reached at dusk. When Mike ordered Lorenzo forward to get the mainsail down he said: 'Do you think I'm fucking stupid?' knowing that this was a phrase used in times of stress but not realising how ripe was the language. Carlo's son Mario followed suit. As a child he had been fascinated by Mike's 'fast and precise' hand. 'Once he drew a Wild West scene, with Indians riding after cowboys, shooting their arrows and the cowboys shooting back with their guns, defending a post coach, the whole thing done in about 15 minutes.'

Mike jet washes *Touchstone* at Downs boatyard, Maldon. Note the step on the aft end of the rudder – it saved two lives

After 30 years of skiing, Mike gave it up at the age of 87. Carlo said: 'He came back early from his last run and remarked in his usual humorous way: "Oh, I think I'll stop skiing, it's just a loss of time."' But it was more profound than that. Skiing had become time lost from sailing – a sport he can still manage.

For many years sailing was something the wounded old soldier Danny Bray could still manage too, and before Mike went off on his skiing jaunts, the pair would sail *Touchstone*, usually leaving the Blackwater on Boxing Day, up the Humber to Winteringham Haven, where Danny would lay her up and carry out any maintenance required. This included fabricating a new dagger board after, while cutting the shoals too fine across Haile Sand Flat entering the Humber Estuary, they grounded and the starboard board snapped in half. Danny also fitted a new engine. 'Danny's advice to me about sailing in the Humber if the tide was against you was: "oog the mod,"' Mike recalled, not that sailing against the Humber tides was often an option: the buoys there are small lightships so as they'll stay afloat.

With Danny Bray, Mike sailed round Britain. He borrowed the charts from author Jonathan Raban who had made the trip earlier in a motor-sailer for his book *Coasting*. 'Some of his phrases were written down the sides of the charts and I thought I must go there and see what it's like. See whether it matches the description,' Mike told me. In Whitby they met another author sailing round Britain in order to write their account of the Sceptred Isle. Libby Purves with her husband Paul Heiney and children were aboard *Grace O'Malley*, their Cornish pilot cutter: a cruise which produced *One Summer's Grace*. As Mike watched a Trinity House vessel

Mike on *Touchstone* at Downs Road Boatyard

lift a giant, weedy and dripping buoy over the deck of Libby's boat before lowering it on the quay. She spotted him, could almost read what was going on in his mind and said: 'You're the last person we want to see at the moment.'

Mike had a surprising phone call around this time from the widow of Alf Thompson, the soldier he'd been in the Italian POW camp with. She told him that Mike had 'kept Alf alive'. This threw Mike as he had always seen Alf as the 'steady one'. It did not puzzle Veronica however. 'Alf Thompson was a soft-spoken, gentle, little man, a solicitor, not the type to put himself forward. Dad was a tough, working class lad who did. He probably got things sorted for him.'

She joined her father for the only Armistice Day parade he ever attended in 2008.

'He went on a whim,' Veronica said, 'and mused how good it would be if Axel was there with his father's Iron Cross. Heinz and dad had been on opposing sides, but got on very well after the war when their children married. Then as we stood in the crowd watching the veterans go by dad heard a little boy ask his mother what a passing soldier got all his medals for. "Killing Germans" dad said, which was an honest if tactless answer.'

What might seem contradictory sentiments was just the truth to Mike. The reality was the war itself; the myth was the Cenotaph, with both sides awarded medals for killing.

Over 60 years of drawing cartoons and age has taken its toll on Mike's eyesight and he now suffers from age-related macular degeneration. The central vision of the retina in his left eye lost its focus although there is still peripheral vision. He was told it was only a question of time before AMD would also affect his right eye. 'I thought I was going to lose my sight,' Mike told me, and he has undergone injections to his left eye at £1,500 a time every six weeks. Fortunately the treatment is now available on the NHS, 'As the government decided it was better to pay for that than have a lot of blind people stumbling about. So I've been lucky. In fact I've been lucky all the way through...'

During the recent economic downturn, Mike – at heart an old socialist – became angry with stories of MP's expenses and drew a cartoon of Big Ben on its side being used as a trough by pig-like Members of Parliament and sent it to Number 10 Downing Street. 'When I read that bankers' bonuses were to be cut I thought Gordon Brown must have got my cartoon,' Mike told me.

• 20 •

Sailing with Mr Peyton

Mike heaved on the block and tackle lifting the heavy dagger board skywards, kicked away a basic wooden chock, which had been taking the weight of the board, then lowered it down flush with the deck. 'Designed by computers,' he said. *Touchstone* now started to grip the River Blackwater and became immediately steerable as I held the shiny horse's head tiller carved for *Touchstone* by Danny Bray.

We had slipped away from Maldon with a light westerly wind just filling a large stripy balloon jib, full main and mizzen.

Abreast of Osea Island, Mike said: 'Time for tea although you've not earned it. How I miss my charterers.' I knew him well enough by now to understand that though his face remained dead-pan he was joking. 'This boat is deliberately labour intensive,' he continued, reminding me that all his Heath-Robinson inventions were born of two very personal necessities: simplicity and task. The former served his own Luddite tendencies the latter the requirement of paying passengers to 'be involved'.

Down below the kettle was whistling and I fished around for the tea. To my horror I found a limp cardboard box with tea bags covered in green mould. I deliberately brought them up on deck and started patting off the dust. To my surprise even Mike was prepared to concede they were an infusion beyond ingestion and he scattered them over the side. "The seagulls'll have 'em" he said mournfully hoping they would not be totally wasted. Not a fowl alighted on the calm river to inspect the floating items in our wake. *Touchstone* is well known to the avian population of Essex.

"HE MUST HAVE ROSE-COLOURED BINOCULARS"

Mike on *Touchstone*, stowing sail...   with drop board...

'Never mind, there's coffee. I forgot the milk, but you take it black and I'm not fussy,' said my skipper.

While researching this book I had become aware that very few warts had surfaced and that it ran the risk of hagiography. It had become a running joke: 'Found any warts yet?' Kath would ask keenly. Now at last I had one, or so I thought. But even the bacteriological weapon in the tea caddy could not be chalked up against Mr Peyton.

It turned out he had a supply of fresh tea bags on board in a screw-top plastic container. The rogue bags were, in fact, just another quiet pointer to his virtue: they belonged to a pleasant fellow who had let our lines go earlier. I later discovered he is an out-of-work actor down on his luck who Mike allows to live aboard *Touchstone* when he isn't sailing her! And that is most of the time these days, for the labour intensiveness is now all Mike's since he no longer charters. 'I couldn't be fussed with all the regulations required these days,' he said. Instead he sails regularly with one of his first charterers who learned to sail aboard *Touchstone* and now has his own boat.

In the very light wind we had, *Touchstone* sailed surprisingly well, especially with the breeze on our beam as we came round into the River Colne and headed up river towards Brightlingsea and its promise of fish and chips: one of Mike's favourite dishes.

It was cold, clear February weather and Mike shipped the coal stove chimney as the sun started dipping below hinterland Essex. I was cheered to see wispy clouds of smoke quickly grow thicker as the 'knobs' of coal caught.

We moored alongside the Brightlingsea floating pontoon and walked to the top of the hard for the fish and chip shop, of great repute – deservedly so as our clean plates proved. By the time we got back it was dark and, as Mike started the engine and I slipped the mooring lines, a figure approached in the night. 'Is Mike aboard?'

with tiller...

with chimney

Mike's Tilley lamp   The coal stove: the heart of all Mike's boats

he asked me, 'Tell him I've caught him sneaking in again. Anyway let him know that if he's going to stay here to watch out for the wind-turbine trot boats which are to-ing and fro-ing all night.' It was the harbourmaster, but we were soon away, sliding into the darkness towards Pyefleet Creek. Our night sight was impaired by the many reflected lights of what appeared to be a floating city but which, as we got closer and picked out its structure through the blaze of shining orbs, was a huge floating crane and two tugs. The floating factory was in for the night, its day's work planting turbines on the Gunfleet Sands over until the morrow.

We nudged up into the sanctuary of Pyefleet and even found a buoy. Its strop was weed covered: always a welcome sign of temporary neglect and it seemed unlikely to be suddenly remembered late on a cold February night.

The only sound below in *Touchstone*'s cave-like interior was the ticking of the chronometer on the main bulkhead and the hissing of the paraffin-fuelled Tilley lamp that Mike had fired up sending choking black fumes into the cabin. Before the contraption actually gave off a steady, hissing light it had produced more flames than an Olympic torch and enough smoke to put the Flying Scotsman to shame.

My bunk was Danny Bray's old berth: right beside the coal stove and I slept warm and snug, if a little kippered from Tilley ignition.

In the morning I watched as Mike made the tea. 'Old North Country habit,' he said as he fished out the tea bag from one mug and dropped it into the second.

'We would get underway before breakfast,' said Mike, 'to give the charterers an appetite. Would you like to do that?' We dropped the mooring and motored further up Pyefleet Creek: it was close to low water and we went on for almost 2 miles. I was surprised just how much space there is in this classic East Coast anchorage, although only for a boat with shoal draught. As we passed the high banks of marsh, Mike recalled a shipwright who knew the names of all the abandoned smacks that once lined the creek. He'd grown up, exploring the creek in his dinghy, and playing in their hulks as a kid. Now many of them have been dug out and restored including the magnificent smack Pioneer. 'He must have had rose-coloured spectacles to see her potential,' said Mike. Eventually we nudged the bottom and here we dropped the kedge anchor, right in among scores of baying brent geese, who kept their distance, and cooked the caviar of cruising: bacon and egg.

A welcome sun shone through the grey morning and as we sailed back down the creek it was all aglitter with sparkles. We passed two men 'punting' their skiff down the inclined muddy bank to the water's edge before we rounded Langenhoe Marsh and headed up the Colne.

The gloriously empty river wound up through rolling wooded hills and suddenly over Geedon Saltings to port a fast-moving cloud of dunlin switch-backed from black, against the sky, to white as they dipped over the marsh, like the waving of a fan.

We carried the young flood up river to Rowhedge where Mike recalled, many years before, how a passing woman caught his mooring line and actually surged it round a bollard. 'I was amazed she knew what to do,' he said. It was the mark of a true saltwater village. We called on his friend Fabian Bush, a shipwright, whose home, draped with the paraphernalia of the sea, stands incongruously cut off from it by a new housing estate, but he was not in residence so we dropped back down river to Wivenhoe and moored alongside a new brick quay, which although fitted with bollards is also fitted with a waist high metal fence on its edge. It is more a promenade for residents than a landing for mariners.

Two pedestrians wandered past, the first looked down at *Touchstone* and said: 'Lovely,' the second, in woolly hat and beard, said: 'They've cut the top of the ladder off,' something we had already discovered about the quayside's steel rungs, 'it's to stop the kids breaking into boats.'

Alongside at Rowhedge on the river Colne. A winter's sail

Mike on the bow of *Touchstone*

Mike was distinctly unimpressed. It would not be the way he would deal with delinquency. 'You've cut your nose off to spite your face,' he said. The wool-hat looked suitably 'Peytoned' and tried to mask his look of mild surprise with a rictus smile before hurrying away.

Over beer in the Rose & Crown on Wivenhoe's old waterfront Mike recalled watching a real life cartoon unfold in front of him from this very pub. A Dutch coaster was nosing up river – and the river here is impossibly narrow – when he came across a fleet of racing dinghies. One of the helmsmen tacked right across the coaster's bow at which point the skipper left the wheel, sat on the rail with his bared buttocks dangling over the side and pretended to defacate on the rogue sailor.

'Difficult one to draw, though, Mike?'

But his mind had already moved on and the talk from Wivenhoe back down river was of self-conducted euthanasia. 'A good way to do it is get in a warm bath of water so you are comfortable, then take sleeping tablets and before you drift off, turn on the cold tap. While you're asleep you die of hypothermia,' Mike said cheerfully.

Interested, I then told him how I'd got talking with two sailing squaddies at Brightlingsea many years ago and they had recommended Semtex coiled round the body: 'You light one end and before you've had time to think about it you're in a million pieces,' they'd said.

Mike has always cherished winter sailing

Mike at navigation table aboard *Touchstone*

That's the beauty of cruising you never know what you'll end up talking about as there are no social mores to worry about out on the water.

We motored down towards Mersea against a chilly south wind and my eyes started to water. Mike was below preparing lunch.

Suddenly a fist thrust out from the companionway holding a steaming roll: 'I hope you like Spam,' came a voice.

I was hungry and wolfed down the bread and its fried filling.

The fist re-appeared with another Spam roll: 'I don't know why people complain about Spam.'

I ate this one, too.

For a third time the hand of plenty appeared bearing Spammed roll: 'I like it,' Mike continued, 'though I think it helps if you eat it outside when *you* are cold and *it* is hot.'

There's only so much Spam you can eat at one standing and the third roll went over the side. I was terrified Mike would come up before it was out of sight and recalled Peter Maynard telling me a similar story involving charterers ditching sausages: to his horror they came drifting back on the young flood

Touchstone off Mersea, Essex

The start of the author's cruise with Mike

and momentarily hung round the boat before moving on, but if Mike had seen them he said nothing.

That night we picked up a buoy in the South Channel which leads up to Tollesbury.

A sly mist crept over the marsh brought in from the North Sea by a light and bitterly cold south-east wind.

'I don't suppose we'll hear the flutin' of the birds tonight,' said Mike as he disappeared in his sleeping bag. I banked up the fire and turned in too. Neither of us were hungry: one of the benefits of Spam, I supposed.

Before dozing off Mike recalled how, when chartering, he would play the popular classics and on one occasion the whole crew noticed how *Touchstone* appeared to be waltzing as she sailed up the Wallet to the strains of the Blue Danube.

Kath had also described to me earlier how while listening to Beethoven's Seventh Symphony in the Pyefleet one summer's evening a pink jellyfish opened and closed just under the surface of the water in time to the maestro's composition.

We lay in our bunks the next morning trying to summon up the enthusiasm to leave them for the chill air of *Touchstone*'s saloon. The knobs of coal in the stove were now perfectly formed balls of ash.

Suddenly Mike said: 'I've been thinking about what's different today from the chartering days and I've worked out that it's me. I've got old. I'm not as energetic.' He then recalled our start from Maldon: how in the old days the boat's bottom would have been clean and not covered with a year's worth of barnacles and weed, how it was a spinnaker breeze – and yet we did not bother setting it – and how, in the old days, he'd have made a night passage and gone down the coast somewhere instead of just chasing Brightlingsea's fish and chips. Also with charterers busying themselves with paintbrushes, deck scrubbers and whipping twine, *Touchstone* would not be as scruffy as she is now.

And certainly the customers had become affectionate towards the old concrete boat even though their holidays were hard work. From the deckhead hung mementoes of their cruises: a winch handle with the legend 'Presented to Mike from the Hernia Section of Sparkhill SC,' 'To the skipper of *Grindstone*' engraved on a plaque, a brass foghorn engraved *Touchstone*. Other bric-a-brac demonstrated just how far afield she travelled: a scallop shell marked Lower Fishguard '89, a Brest '92 plaque, an oyster shell engraved Blakeney '81. A group of railwaymen from Crewe engine sheds went back to work, after a charter aboard *Touchstone*, with an order for a heavy gauge copper frying pan which would fit across both Primus burners. They came back the following summer and Mike has the pan to this day.

Mike moors *Touchstone* up to a Thames sailing barge at Hythe Quay, Maldon

With her utilitarian appearance, wherever *Touchstone* went she was hailed by other mariners seeking tools. A fisherman greeted them in Fishguard: 'Have you got a wrench? You look like the sort of boat which has a wrench' – she does. In Yarmouth a yachtsman asked, 'Do you have a saw? You look like the sort of boat which might,' Mike proudly offered them two.

We slipped the anchor and motored out through the shoal creek of South Channel to pick up the early flood at the Nass Beacon to take us back up the Blackwater. There was fog in the river but eventually the dark square blocks of Bradwell Power Station pieced themselves together in the murk and gave us a fix.

'If it was foggy I'd say to the charterers: "Oh what luck, now we can test our navigational skills". I mean, if they'd come all the way from the Midlands you couldn't just sit about,' said Mike as we drifted towards Stone Point in the mist. "I'd have one on the bow as lookout, one casting the lead and another one steering.' If there was no wind these poor charterers would be engaged in the act of 'drudging': using the tide to move the boat and dropping the anchor so as its crown would just touch the sea-bed and bring her head to tide before heaving up and setting off once more. Yet they kept coming back for more!

By the time we reached Maldon we were early on the tide and moored alongside the sailing barge *Kitty* at Hythe Quay. We went ashore for a pint beside a blazing log fire in the Queen's Head to await more flood.

We left *Touchstone* in her mud berth and drove back to Rookery Cottage where Kath made us tea.

'Do you have all the safety gear for such important guests as Dick?' she asked half-mocking, half serious.

Mike remained expressionless.

"ACCORDING TO THIS SERVICE-BY DATE, ONLY ANOTHER YEAR AND YOU'LL
HAVE A CLASSIC LIFERAFT AS WELL"

'That bloody liferaft I bought you for your birthday is 10 years old and hasn't been serviced since you got it. Has it? You can put that in the book, Dick.'

Mike remained silent.

'And as for saying you don't need it on deck because the adrenaline rush of a man on a sinking boat would get it out quickly is nonsense. What adrenaline have you got at the age of nearly ninety?'

Mike sipped his tea.

'The adrenaline rush of a man who's nearly ninety on a boat made of cement...she'd sink like a stone. Yachting is very dangerous...'

'But not as dangerous as riding,' said Mike with impeccable timing.

• *Index* •